INTO THE LIGHT

A MEMOIR

ELIZABETH ROBERTSON

Copyright © Elizabeth Robertson 2023

First published in Australia in 2023

Conker Productions

ISBN

Large Print Paperback: 978-0-6456983-0-5

Paperback: 978-0-6456983-3-6

Ebook: 978-0-6456983-1-2

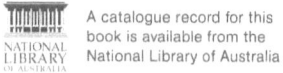
A catalogue record for this book is available from the National Library of Australia

All rights reserved.

No part of this book may be reproduced in any form or by any electronic or mechanical means, including information storage and retrieval systems, without written permission from the author, except for the use of brief quotations in a book review.

Managing editor: Belinda Pollard

Proofreader: Alix Kwan

Cover design by Belinda Pollard

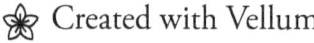 Created with Vellum

One cannot meet Beth Robertson without sensing something *different*—a difference born of the Spirit of God and a relationship to Him made possible through Jesus Christ. Told with wit and pathos, and her trademark honesty, the stories in these pages testify to that difference, together with the *hope* and *joy* that have carried Beth through some truly remarkable transitions. May her story move you deeply, the way Beth herself has moved all those fortunate enough to have met her.

James Cooper
Head of Creative Writing & Communication,
Tabor Adelaide

Into the Light is an inspiring and fascinating memoir, brimming with love, peace and humour, a true story of spiritual growth and transformation. It portrays a wise and beautiful life lived in a constant desire to seek relationship with God. From racial ostracisation as a child and having little sense of identity, the young Beth grows from fear to faith and giving thanks in all circumstances, whether it be nursing in Australia or Sudan, singleness or marriage. What startling stories of being found by God's love, healings and of miracles! Beth points out that as you grow closer to the light the more spots show, but I discovered that Beth's light, reflected from her Lord, shone out brightly to all she met. This life story could easily sit beside Patricia St John's memoir.

Dr Rosanne Hawke
Author
Former Creative Writing lecturer, Tabor Adelaide

CONTENTS

Prologue	1
1. Where do I belong?	9
2. Learning new things	33
3. From schoolgirl to nurse	50
4. Call the midwife	70
5. Preparation for Africa	78
6. From Khartoum to Chali el Fil	93
7. Rescue by donkey and shank's pony	109
8. From Chali el Fil to Abaiyat	126
9. Leaving home, coming home	143
10. A partner in the dance	156
11. Retreat to the country	168
12. Encounter	176
13. Beginning a new journey	182
14. Adelaide anecdotes	191
15. A turning point	198
16. Heartbroken but homeward bound	209
About the Author	221

If you and I have known each other it is most probable that you have read, helped, inspired and corrected my writing significantly.
Your name should be included in any list of acknowledgements—the problem being that the list might well be longer than the book.
Please accept my grateful thanks.

PROLOGUE

That evening was flawless. The blue sky soared to infinity, the radiant sun dipped its toes into the tranquil sea, as I stood at the rail of the ocean liner clutching a handful of multi-coloured streamers. The quiet throbbing of the engine quickened. The ship moved majestically away from the wharf. The last streamer drifted disconsolately in the water, and the familiar faces of those left behind blurred beyond recognition.

Standing at the ship's rail and shivering a little in the cooling air, my thoughts were chaotic. The widening gap between ship and shore symbolised for me the changes taking place in my life. Excitement as I looked forward to the new life ahead of me warred with the sadness of separation from home and loved ones. Above all,

I could never forget the wounded look in my mother's deep blue eyes.

The year was 1954. I was twenty-eight years old and on my way to begin a four-year term in the Sudan, East Africa, as a missionary with the Sudan Interior Mission. Seven years of preparation lay behind me, with qualifications in general nursing, midwifery, child welfare and Bible study.

Immersed in my reveries, I jumped when a voice behind me boomed, 'Hello! You must be Beth Wordie.'

I turned to find a tall young man with rampant red hair and a cheerful freckled face smiling at me. My hand disappeared in his as we shook hands.

'Yes, I'm Beth, and you must be Richard.'

A diminutive woman, who looked to be about my age, popped out from behind Richard saying, 'I'm June.'

'We thought we'd give you some time by yourself before we came looking for you,' added Richard. 'I came aboard in Sydney, and June joined the ship in Melbourne.'

'Thanks for finding me. I was mightily relieved when the Mission told me that you would be my fellow travellers. I even studied your photos to be sure I'd recognise you. You see, I've never been outside Australia before.'

'Me either,' said June. 'How about you, Richard?'

'Same as you two, and although I'm looking forward to going to Ethiopia it will be a year before my fiancée comes to join me. I'm certainly going to miss her,' answered Richard wistfully.

'You're going to the Sudan, aren't you, Beth?' said June.

'Yes, which means I'll be saying goodbye to you both when we get to Aden. I'm flying to Khartoum from there.'

A clamorous gong interrupted our meeting with its summons to dinner. With a final backward glance at the lights of Adelaide as they shone out in the darkening sky, I turned towards my new life.

Richard, June and I soon became good friends. Apart from being ejected from the community area when our uproarious game of Scrabble interfered with Housie Housie—aka Bingo—we kept a low profile… until our tender consciences forced us to follow the instructions of 'the book'!

'The book' was the Sudan Interior Mission's guide for the behaviour of its missionaries while on board ship. It had been written in the 1800s and said, in effect:

> The tropical sun is very dangerous. Therefore, when you near the equator you must put on your pith helmets whenever you walk on deck.

If you have seen pictures of David Livingstone, you would probably recognise a pith helmet: usually white, formal, hard, held in place by a leather strap under the chin, and still worn by some officials in the tropics.

The fateful day dawned. June and I smuggled our helmets into Richard's cabin, donned them, tightened the unrelenting leather straps under our chins, and, in a hesitant huddle with Richard as our leader, stepped onto the deck where throngs of carefree people paraded, played games, or lay draped over deck chairs. Most of them flaunted colourful, stylish clothing with little attempt to cover their exquisitely bronzed skins.

How ridiculous we must have looked in our modest clothing surmounted by pith helmets!

After a moment's stunned silence in which it seemed that every person within eyeshot inhaled a synchronised, incredulous breath, it started. Hoots, catcalls, raucous laughter—orchestrated by a group of dissatisfied 'Poms' on their way back to Britain after failed attempts at immigration.

Now you *might* have predicted that as embryonic missionaries given an unexpected opportunity to exhibit the spirit of the early martyrs, we would have marched on bravely, smiling sweetly, undeterred by the ribaldry around us. But you would have been wrong! We fell over each other in our efforts to escape the assault. The pith helmets were buried in the depths of our luggage and next greeted the light of day where they belonged, in Africa.

By the time the ship reached Aden, shipboard life had become happy and familiar, and my travelling companions were like family to me.

MY FAVOURITE PLACE on board ship was by the rail, overlooking the sea, as far forward as possible, and I discovered such a spot where, soothed by the swishing of the sea, I marvelled at the dexterity of the dolphins and the flamboyance of the flying fish as they gambolled and soared around the sharp prow of the ship as it cut its path through the waves. There was plenty of time for me to reflect on the past and pray and ponder about the future.

My feelings about leaving Adelaide were mixed. On one hand, sadness for my mother, nearly seventy, living alone; the four-year term seemed so long, and the Sudan was regarded as a dangerous place to live. On the other hand, I believed God had called me to work there.

'Please God,' I had prayed, 'close the door if I am mistaken.' Far from being closed, the door had been flung wide open as money flooded in for my support, together with the items needed to furnish my home in Africa, including the four years' supply of toilet paper.

An Almighty God could certainly care for all concerns and the safest place to be, for any of us, must be where He leads.

It was from the vantage point by the ship's rail that I first glimpsed the continent of Africa, dark, distant and mantled in mist. For the first time in my life, I felt a connection with my paternal grandfather, Vaules Wordie, whose ancestors had been born in this land.

Ships, or the lack of them, had been essential to my parents meeting each other.

Vaules had made an incredible journey from Jamaica, the land of slavery, to begin a new life in the relatively new colony of Adelaide, South Australia. There he met and married Englishwoman Ada Clamp, who would give birth to my father, Herbert, in 1894.

Another ship, the *Osterley*, carried the fervently patriotic English woman, Lily King, to Adelaide for a holiday with her uncle. The outbreak of World War I and the consequent lack of shipping kept her there, where she and Herbert were married. She was actually on the train to

Outer Harbour to board the ship for England when World War I was declared.

My own life story began on October the ninth, 1926 in the Memorial Hospital, Adelaide, as a scrawny, sickly baby suffering from pneumonia, weighing five and a half pounds and with a tenuous hold on life. My future was definitely in the balance. As I look back over my ninety-four years, I can only conclude that 'with God all things are possible'.

There are many ways to regard our lives. Some see life as a series of random events. I used to think this way in my pompous teens when I knew almost everything! But after a close encounter with Jesus Christ I came to see my life as a tapestry, with multi-coloured threads from many directions being woven by God my Father into a pattern for His purposes.

1

WHERE DO I BELONG?

At a very early age, I was bewildered by the way people treated me. I was somehow different from other people, and that difference was shameful. People stared at me, pointed at me, whispered about me, asked to look at my fingernails and spoke strange words that no-one would explain to me—like half-caste, coon, nigger and blackfella. I gathered that this problem was somehow associated with my father.

I was walking home from school alone, as usual. The year was 1933 and I was in Grade 2 at school. Just in front of me walked a girl whose name I have forgotten but whom I will call Dora —the best-dressed, bossiest girl in the class!

As we walked along, I suddenly spied on the pavement ahead a shiny threepenny piece. These were the days of the Great Depression and my father was unemployed. Threepence was a fortune to me.

If only Dora doesn't see it, it'll be mine, I said to myself, crossing my fingers and holding my breath. Unbelievably, she walked right over it. Triumphantly I swooped down and scooped it up, boasting, 'Look! I found threepence!'

At this, Dora spun around, her flaxen pigtails flying, spluttering, 'That's *my* threepence. Give it to me!'

'It's not yours,' I retorted. 'You walked right over the top of it.'

'I *always* walk over the top of something before I pick it up,' replied Dora. But I refused to give in. Petulantly, Dora turned on her heel and flounced off home.

I breathed again, dreaming of the sweets this money would buy.

But a lot can happen overnight.

The following day, Dora came to class with a letter from her parents, claiming that I had stolen her threepence. Her claims were accepted without question, and I went home with a letter to my parents, demanding the coin's return.

Although my father believed my story and wrote a letter of protest, it was ignored. The teacher called out Dora and me to stand in front of the class, and I was told to return 'Dora's threepence'.

A triumphant Dora snatched the coin. The

teacher smiled. No-one ever asked me what happened.

My father, Herbert, was handsome, strong, talented and proud, with an excellent singing and speaking voice and courteous ways, though he was a strict disciplinarian to me.

His mixed racial heritage was a great disadvantage in a society which adhered with pride to the White Australia Policy.

In 1916, World War I was at its bloodiest when Bert, as my dad was nicknamed, enlisted in the army. He was just nineteen years old. Before he left for France, there was a hasty marriage to my mother, Lillian.

Lillian, or Lily as she was often called, was a small woman, slight, with such beautiful blue-violet eyes that a painter used her as a model. Normally truthful, she vehemently declared she was five feet tall, knowing very well that she was a mere four foot eleven. She had never expected or wanted to live in Australia. She had merely come to visit an uncle.

Born in a small English village, the seventh child in a family of eight, her father's accident and invalidism resulted in her working as a 'tweeny', a junior maid, in London at the age of fourteen. Following a broken engagement and her father's death, when she was twenty-eight she came for a holiday with her mother and sister to Adelaide in 1914 to visit an uncle.

Lillian 'Lily' King

She was about to return home to England when her uncle was knocked down by a horse and killed. The shock led to her mother's death a week later from a stroke. Lillian and her sister Beatrice, in the midst of their grief, felt the relief of homecoming to be finally returning to England at last. They were actually on a train bound for Outer Harbour to board a ship when World

War I broke out. All ships were requisitioned for war purposes. Lily was trapped in Australia. She returned to Adelaide and married Herbert in 1916 on the eve of his departure to France as a soldier.

I can only imagine her sense of bereavement as she waved goodbye to her new husband. It would be three years before they met again.

By the time the couple were reunited in 1920, both had been victims of traumatic experiences. Bert's horrific war service in France had bequeathed a legacy of depression and fearful nightmares. Lillian's loneliness in a foreign country, coupled with her anxiety for her husband, had contributed to the worsening of her depressive disorder.

The joy of reunion faded fast, in the face of my mother's determination to remain childless because of the problems for someone of mixed race. Although my birth in 1926 was a tragedy from her viewpoint, my frailty—I had been born with pneumonia—touched her heart. 'I didn't change my clothes for a fortnight,' she later told me. She saved my life.

After demobilisation, Bert qualified as an engineering draughtsman and was employed by the railways. He was due to be promoted to permanent employment a week or two before the Great Depression erupted and all such entitlements were abolished. He was, instead, part of the great multitude of the unemployed. I once heard his desperate sobbing. He sought work tirelessly, without success.

Herbert 'Bert' Wordie

He designed the complicated cages for the Adelaide Zoo. Orangutans were sent to the zoo only after the cages had been approved by the donor nation. He also acted as architect for several friends, drawing up plans and writing the specifications for their homes. At home, he grew vegetables and made a splendid garden.

My parents' expressions of anger were in stark contrast—my mother's explosive and hysterical, my father's icily cold. I used to think my mother, like the phoenix, rose from the flames. I found my father easier to get on with, although his long silences when offended were difficult to bear. He and his mother had not spoken to each other for twenty years and I met her only once, a wispy, wrinkled little woman with piercing, hostile dark eyes; it was obvious that her dislike of my parents extended to me.

I loathed the racial heritage from my dad, in which I perceived hurt, rejection and shame. I struggled with my feelings of resentment towards him, coupled with guilt for feeling that way.

Prior to 1930 or thereabouts, our financial circumstances were promising. My Dad went off to work daily. At the end of the day, I would be there watching at the window, waiting to run to the gate to meet him and be swept up in his arms for a hug.

Friday nights were especially important. I would see the shape in his right-hand pocket and knew what it meant: an Old Gold chocolate. We were in for a feast.

A young Beth Wordie (R) with her cousin Peter Barker

My life as a small child would have been less controversial had it not been for the popularisation by Mrs Amelia Bloomer of the garments henceforth known by her name. In my day, bloomers were akin to pantaloons, elasticised around the waist and upper legs. They provided a wonderful receptacle for things you wanted to hide. Burnt crusts disappeared and your parents congratulated themselves. So much more peaceful—that is, if you could dispose of the evidence.

On Christmas Eve in a shop with my mother, I saw the most entrancing glass bottle filled with silver balls for cake decoration. I couldn't help myself. Quick as a flash my hand darted out, and with one smooth movement the bottle was securely stowed away in my bloomers.

We were home before the frightening question came to me. What was I going to do now? We were a regular family of that day, in that my father ruled with the razor strop (a thick leather belt used for sharpening razors) and my mother wielded the wooden spoon. I was never bruised but it wasn't enjoyable.

Suddenly, a brilliant thought came: just add it to Santa's gifts and no-one would be any the wiser.

Imagine my disappointment next morning to discover that Santa had dobbed me in.

On another occasion I found a stone that looked just like a tooth and set it up, but the tooth fairy let me down too.

THE GREAT DEPRESSION arrived and my Dad's promised permanent job disappeared, along with most of our assets. Dad rarely smiled in those days.

The local Methodist church provided important spiritual, social and practical support during those years—services, fetes, sports events, music concerts, without which our lives would have been much more drab and depressive.

On one occasion the church members planned a community fishing day. Shortly after dawn, fifteen fishing boats set sail. These were the 'hungry years' of the Great Depression, and my father was more anxious than most to bring something home for dinner.

I had learned to pray with faith and had often seen answers. 'Please, please God, help my dad to catch fish,' I prayed, many times.

Towards evening we went down to the shore to welcome the fishermen home. As they splashed through the water it was obvious from the downcast looks that it had not been a good day.

Then we saw my dad, his fishing bag riding heavily on his shoulder and a smile on his face.

I can still visualise the three very large snapper, their scales rimed with salt, their large yellow and black eyes so still. Large enough to have some to eat and some to sell.

When I began to pray for a tricycle for Christmas, my mother was not encouraging. From her point of view there was no possibility, human or divine. It was hard enough to provide the necessities of life.

'You must not be greedy,' she cautioned.

Secretly, a few days later, a neighbour, Mrs

Flint, whose family owned a large store in Hindley Street, beckoned Mum, and asked if Mum would like a tricycle for me.

I remember Christmas morning. 'Come outside, Beth. I've something to show you.'

It must have been too big to go down the chimney. I have never forgotten the brilliance of that newly painted silver and scarlet bike that outshone the sun.

'See, Mum,' I was said to have remarked, 'God does answer prayer.' I was probably five years old at the time. At ninety-four I say the same thing with the greatest conviction.

Just before I started school, my mother and I were enjoying a visit to Henley Beach, my favourite place in the whole world. I loved the beach and the sea, but even better was the enormous wooden slippery dip. I would climb the wooden stairs, hanging on to the rail until I reached the top, and wait my turn in the fenced platform large enough to hold half a dozen children. Eventually my turn would come to step forward and sit down, anticipating the dizzy bliss of the wind in my hair and the blur of the passing landscape.

Because of the height of the platform—about

six feet—there would frequently be a supervising adult nearby... but not on this day.

I clearly recall climbing a third of the way up the stairs and seeing a group of children in the enclosure at the top of the slide, but remember nothing more until I regained consciousness. I was lying on the sand beneath the platform with my head against a wooden pole, having obviously reached the top and somehow fallen or been pushed. I looked up at the pitiless faces of the children of various ages peering down at me from the platform and heard their jeering voices. No-one offered to help me.

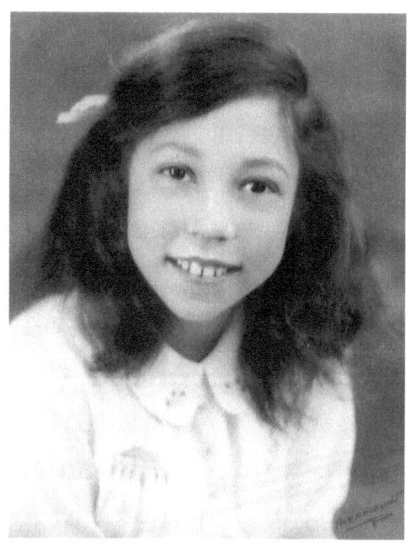

Beth as a young schoolgirl

Although dazed, I managed to get up and run to find my mother, who remained unaware of my fall or of the concussion I had apparently suffered.

My mother dreaded the day that I would have to go to school, and kept me at home until I was six years old. I don't remember my first day at school but, before long, each school day became a battle.

I was decidedly left-handed, but it was the decision of the school—and my mother—that students be forced to be right-handed. I clutched the pencil so tightly a lump developed on my third finger. Handy, too—I could always tell my right hand by feeling for the lump.

When the headmaster decided to give a monetary prize to the 'tallest girl in the class', why was it was given to Margaret, who was so obviously shorter than I? Didn't I count as a person?

I tried to hold back tears and pretended not to care that I was always last to be picked for games. Why couldn't they see that I was really good at sport? Then one day a boy actually picked me first for a game. Oh, the joy of the occasion! I am still grateful to him, and have warmed my spiritual hands many times at the memory of that small fire.

One frightening day stands out in my memory. Looking ahead, I could see a group of my classmates standing on a rise alongside the footpath in the shadow of a great pine tree. They held stones in their hands and were being urged on by an older boy wearing a white hat. I have never felt more fearful or more alone as I did that day as stones fell on me and around me while hate-filled voices chanted 'nigger'.

As I arrived home, shaky and sobbing, and snuggled into my mother's outstretched arms, I heard her despairing whisper: 'You poor little thing, you should never have been born.'

MY EARLIEST MEMORY is of my mounting hysteria as I tried to stop my parents from shouting at one another, begging them to 'kiss and be friends'. Mercifully, I never saw any physical violence, but the friction between them became so fierce at times that my father would sometimes come and kiss me goodnight and just walk out into the darkness, not returning for hours, or days. I didn't know where he went.

Whenever this occurred, my mother could become depressed, irrational, and even suicidal. From the age of eight until my teens, there were times I chased after her through the darkness of night, crying and pleading with her, as she ran towards the beach threatening to throw herself off the jetty. There were times when I slept under the bed hoping she would not find me and punish me as she had threatened; or I would gaze in horror as she feigned madness.

'They will put me in Parkside'—the infamous mental hospital—'and I'll just sit there playing with a piece of string,' she would say, her face terribly contorted like a mad woman.

In my distress once, I wrote a tear-stained note to my father, who had kissed me before leaving: 'Your goodnight kiss was the last happy thing I knew.' However, I never talked to him or anyone else about the situation, and my father only learned a very little of my side of the story many years later, after my mother's death. 'I thought you got on well with her,' he said.

Eventually, the situation grew so bad between my parents that Dad left home. But he always supported my mother and me financially, to some extent. Eighteen months after he left home, he was part of a syndicate that won money in a lottery, with which he bought the Westbourne Park house where my mother and I lived. What a blessing that was to us, and I am sure in my own mind that Dad's win was part of the Lord's loving plan for us although we didn't realise it at the time.

I read recently in Madeleine L'Engle's book *Walking on Water* that she and her husband believed the best gift they could give their children was the demonstration of their love for each other. I am sure that statement is true, and tried to recall whether I had ever seen either of my parents express love for each other, but I couldn't. My heart is still sad for their loss, and for mine.

I AM SO grateful for my mother's determination to rescue me, with much struggling and sacrifices, which included selling family heirlooms and anything else of value.

She succeeded in sending me to Methodist Ladies College (MLC), Wayville (now Annesley Junior School), for three years. Bullying was no longer a problem, but poverty and discrimination due to my mixed-race heritage remained. It was years before I understood my introduction to the class by Miss McMutrie: 'This is Elizabeth who, because she comes from a race of people who are unsettled and who go walkabout, will find it hard to sit in class and to study.' It was also years before I understood why she scolded me for being ignorant of the nature of saltbush, which had apparently saved the lives of 'my people'. I puzzled over it for some time. When I did meet an Indigenous Australian girl some years later, I envied her. She had an identity and a country and a race, whereas I was nobody from nowhere.

When I was twelve, my mother could no longer afford the school fees and I left the MLC for Unley High School. As the Great Depression had deepened, we had lost many valuable items from our home, including precious antiques my mother had brought from England. My mother regularly pawned her pretty gold engagement ring with the three diamonds, to provide food for us—until the next dole cheque arrived and she could redeem it. But one day she came home sobbing. Her ring had been sold. She was heartbroken. It symbolised everything she had lost: her beloved country, family and self-respect. She was inconsolable.

Australia would always be a foreign land to Mother. She spoke longingly of England, of the woods spangled with dew-decked daffodils and violets, and the fragrance of new-mown hay. From the time I was a little child I used to dream: *When I grow up, I am going to get some money and buy her a ticket for England.* The time came, years later, when this became possible and I anticipated her joy when I went to her saying, 'Mum, good news, I've saved enough to buy you a ticket for England. You can see the woods with the daffodils and violets and smell the new-mown hay again.'

Her eyes filled with tears as she replied bitterly, 'It's too late now. I'd only be visiting graveyards.'

I realised, then, how sad and lonely her life had been, and wished I could make it up to her. I held her in my arms and cried with her.

ONE OF MY mother's favourite sayings was, 'Blessed is he who expecteth nothing, for verily he shall not be disappointed.' I seconded this philosophy. Afraid to hope, I too anticipated disappointment and failure, and developed a strange sort of coping mechanism. Because success was impossible for me, it would be best not to try. At least that way I could find some small degree of comfort in knowing I could have done better, rather than having to face the fact that I was utterly hopeless.

Consequently, I never received a good school report. Without exception, each said in one way or another, 'Beth could do better if she tried.' And that gave me comfort. I took a kind of perverse pride in preserving my position—about third place from the bottom of the class. I devoted any serious attention to devouring story books or playing sport, at which I actually excelled (though in those days this didn't count for much).

I came to resemble a chameleon, having no sense of my own identity. I coveted acceptance, and tried to become what each person I met wanted me to be. This led to disillusionment from my friends and acquaintances, who were repelled by my disloyalty.

Naturally, my mother was very disappointed

with my lack of success. As I grew older I would join her in her mantra, which went like this: 'I have worked my fingers to the bone for you and you have let me down all the way along the line.' We would laugh, then, but Mum had given up a lot for me. I'm glad she lived long enough to see rewards in my life for her struggles to give me a good education.

Another of my mother's sayings, 'donkeys are better led than driven', infers that I was very stubborn, and that certainly was (and probably still is) one of my faults.

IN MY FIRST year at high school, my domestic arts teacher, Miss Johnstone, ordered me to apologise to her for something I hadn't done—and have now forgotten.

'Apologise to me immediately!' she demanded.

'But I didn't do it, so I can't apologise,' I quavered—not in defiance but according to my primitive sense of logic.

'Very well, Beth, you will report to me every afternoon after school until you apologise.'

'Yes, Miss Johnstone.'

I had no idea that this was putting Miss Johnstone under stress, and cheerfully reported to her for the next three afternoons. Feeling oddly important to be noticed by a teacher, I would have been happy to continue the practice indefinitely.

I was incredulous, therefore, when Miss Finn, my regular class teacher, whom I really liked, called me aside after class one day and said, 'Poor Miss Johnstone is really upset, and you know she has not been very well. I would really appreciate it if you apologised to her.'

'Alright, Miss Finn,' I assured her. 'I'll try.'

I thought it over carefully and finally approached the teacher, saying, 'Miss Johnstone, I'm very sorry you were upset because you thought I did something wrong. I promise not to do it again.'

I knew I would never understand teachers when at this she dissolved into tears and gave me a big hug. It was rather comforting.

At school I became a survivor. Often trying to hide my tears, I would act as if unmoved by rejection or teasing and would lie, steal and cheat to escape trouble. My consequent guilt and despair led to self-hatred. I walked around whispering, *I hate myself, I hate myself, I hate myself.* I don't think I blamed anyone else. No, I was a wicked person who deserved it. I have often thought in later years that a large part of this attitude was due to my situation as an only child—I just didn't know that other children behaved at home the same way I did.

The difficulties I faced growing up—struggling to fit in to my world while also trying to cope with my parents' turbulent relationship—strengthened my belief that my life was an unfortunate mistake. I'm sure I was not the first child to have harboured such self-doubt, and I am thankful that despite several instances of sexual harassment, I was spared the extreme physical and sexual abuse that is still endured by so many children.

Life was indeed problematic, but I was blessed by the joy of music and literature, which my parents introduced me to when I was very young. Both my mum and dad sang to me, and I apparently sang before I talked. Sleep time was preceded by a story and prayer.

Mother, a gifted raconteur, painted living pictures of her childhood and the idyllic beauty of her homeland. Bluebells and daffodils had spangled the fields with blue and gold near her English village. Her memories were revived of long-gone birds that sang, and squirrels that scampered to and fro, harvesting nuts. I was sure that I smelled the woodsy perfume of violets and delighted in the trembling brilliance of dewdrops. Mother attributed these things to God the Creator, and taught me to pray to Him. These gifts now form blessed foundations for my Christian life view.

The most influential nonfiction literature I remember as a young child was from the Bible. I devoured the stories, which I learned to read in a simplified form. I loved the bright stories of Jesus but sorrowed over the crucifixion. I told my mother, 'I wish I was there with my hanky to wipe away the blood from His face.' Stories set to music as hymns and choruses opened my heart and taught me of the love of God. My favourite was the second verse of the hymn *When I Read That Sweet Story of Old*.

> Oh, I wish that His hands had been placed on my head,
> That His arm had been thrown around me
> And that I could have seen His kind look when He said,
> 'Let the little ones come unto me.'

It was as if I felt the actual touch of the Lord. Warmth enveloped my being, teaching me to appreciate the good and lovely aspects of life, and giving me faith to believe that God would answer my prayer.

My mother read *Little Women* to me, repeatedly, long before I could read it for myself. Later,

I continued to read it again and again for myself. I soon learned that I had been named Beth for one of the book's characters, which gave me a sense of identity with the character and her family. Multiple rereadings of the story also gave me a sense of permanence that was lacking in my life: my parents' tumultuous relationship had deteriorated so that by the time I was twelve years old, my father had left home; we had moved house nine times by the time I was thirteen years old; and my mother's bouts of suicidal depression had worsened. The lonelier I felt, the more I turned to reading books like *Little Women* and the *Anne of Green Gables* series.

Little Women was the textbook from which I learned many things: family love, gratitude, compassion for the poor, the advisability of truthfulness, the dangers of unforgiveness, the sadness of death, and the importance of controlling one's tongue and one's temper. I still recall the episodes that illustrated these points, which became the keyholes through which I observed family life. As a solitary 'only child' I played innumerable competitive games of hopscotch and skipping, pretending to be each of the March sisters in turn (there was a strong probability that 'Beth' would win). How I longed to be part of such a family. Although not ideal, the knowledge gained from literature formed an irreplaceable aspect of my upbringing.

Circumstances improved for my mother and me with the advent of World War II. Suddenly, there was work for everyone. Young people joined up, or took the jobs left vacant when the men joined the forces. My mother, then in her fifties, found a job at a munitions factory. She bought new furniture, crystal glassware, a pretty tulip dinner set, rugs for the floor and a bicycle for me. I was very pleased—the mile walk to school had been tedious. I could forget the shame at MLC when I had only my sports uniform to wear to the fancy dress party, where I pretended to be a Roman soldier! I no longer needed to wear my school uniform to church.

2

LEARNING NEW THINGS

As a teenager, I considered myself an expert on church and Christianity. For as long as I could remember, I had been a prolific but lukewarm church attender—four services every Sunday. If anyone had tried to tell me that prayer and worship could be interesting and important in my life, I would never have believed them. Our family—Mum, Dad and I—were always at church, but as far as I could see we were no happier for it, so I put those thoughts out of my mind.

The best thing about church, as far as I was concerned, was its value as a social club. I had my own escape mechanisms to endure the tedium of sermons—short anecdotal homilies exhorting one to be good and kind. I learned that counting the cracks in the ceiling, the pipes in the organ, or the panes in the stained-glass windows made the time pass more quickly. And the agony was compensated for by the fun and games—various concerts, fetes and Sunday School picnics that sprang up on a regular basis. There were important perks attached to church attendance in the Great Depression era: social and sporting activities unaffordable elsewhere. It was cheap, too: just sixpence a week in the collection plate.

One day my mother mistakenly contributed a Ludo boardgame token—much to her embarrassment, and to the consternation of the richest man in the district who collected the plate from her. I never saw my mum make a faster exit from church than she did that day! Oh, except the day, still a vague memory, when I was dragged from the church singing, 'Hallelujah!'

IN MY EARLY TEENS, my life became a battlefield. Something deep within me cried out to be good, and to know the 'gentle Shepherd' to whom I had prayed nightly. As a child, I was certain of his loving care and protection. Though I turned over many new leaves, trying to be a better person, each new start became, like my school copybooks, blotted and stained. Religion, it seemed, was just another arena of failure for me.

At high school, I was introduced to science, and especially the theory of evolution. I soon began to question the literal truth of the Bible. We had never opened the Bible at home, and all I really knew were a few texts picked up from sermons, and the Bible stories like Daniel and the lions' den.

Our religious instructor at school, the head in Adelaide of one of the popular denominations, taught us that much of the Bible consisted of myths suited to a prescientific people. He said it should not be referred to as 'the Word of God' by people living in the twentieth century. We should say instead that it 'contained the word of God'—just as gold is found in ore. He advised us that because we now know the truth about our world as proven by science, we should, by using the mental processes of our minds, discard the unscientific rubbish in the Bible—such as the accounts of miracles and of creation.

I pondered over these things. With the typical know-it-all outlook of a self-important teenager, I likened humankind to colonies of insignificant ants performing the same dreary futile tasks day by day, each individual struggling and straining to become the top ant. Big deal!

Like many others of my age at that time, I revelled in Keats' poetry and other woeful writings, luxuriating mournfully in the misery of human existence. Atheism beckoned seductively as an expression of rebellion and intellectual freedom, an escape from superstition and old-fashioned ideas.

One day in September, just before my sixteenth birthday, I noticed a pamphlet in the library at school. A Christian organisation, the Children's Special Service Mission (which would later become Scripture Union), was inviting students to a Christian camp to be held during the September school holidays at an Anglican retreat and conference house at Belair, in the Adelaide hills.

Although I was dubious about the Christian element, most of the program excited me: games, sports, sausage sizzles, charades. A holiday away from home involving fun and games far outweighed my niggling doubts. I was, after all, the survivor of a million sermons, and my exceptional gift for selective deafness was indisputable. There was very little fun in my life. I absolutely had to get to this camp.

Breathless with excitement, I pedalled hard all the way home from school, threw open the door, and raced to find my mother, who was in the kitchen, cleaning the stove.

'Mum, I've got something really important to ask you. Please listen!' I blurted breathlessly.

My mother put down the Brasso and her cleaning cloth, looking at me resignedly as I perched on the kitchen stool and began to explain.

'There's going to be this kind of camp for girls in the September holidays, at Belair. It'll be lots of fun and games, and we can talk about schoolwork and all! Can I go? Please? Please say yes. Please, Mum!'

'Now slow down, Beth,' my mother began. 'I can't say anything until I know more about it.' She paused, and added, 'How much is it going to cost?'

For a moment my heart sank. Before my mother went to work in the munitions factory we would never have been able to afford such a treat. Thankfully, before I got too upset, I noticed a smile on Mum's face, and I crossed my fingers hoping for a yes.

Over the next couple of weeks, we collected and checked off everything on the list of requirements—or so we thought. On the night before the camp, as we took a final look at the list, we found with dismay we'd missed something. Mum was the first to notice it.

'That's a bit strange,' she commented. 'They want you to take a Bible. Your dad used to have one, but I've no idea where it is. Go and look in the spare room.'

I dashed off to check—no luck. Then, between us, we ransacked the rest of the house. We could not find a Bible anywhere.

'What'll I do, Mum?' I wailed, terrified that she might change her mind about my going to the camp.

What a relief when she said, 'Oh, don't worry. It can't be very important. Can it?'

'Of course not,' I agreed.

AND SO I arrived at the retreat and conference house in Belair with my suitcase, minus one Bible. My roommate and I named the high-ceilinged room we shared in the once-elegant mansion the 'Flowery Bower' in honour of the pale blue, pink-blossom-bedecked wallpaper.

Almost immediately, I felt a difference in the atmosphere. There was a calming absence of stress at the camp. People seemed happy, and related to each other as if they were part of a loving family. If only I could stay here forever…

I thoroughly enjoyed the camp atmosphere and activity programs, trying to ignore as much as possible the Christian content. My early atheistic leanings were greatly challenged, particularly by the miracles of creation that I saw around me in the hills. Evolution no longer satisfied me, and I made the momentous decision to believe in God the Creator. But there was no way I could accept the virgin birth, or believe that Jesus was 'God's only begotten Son'!

For some crazy reason, I thought that by renouncing my atheistic view of the world and accepting the concept of God on my own terms, I had somehow become a Christian! I was really happy for at least three days after I returned home.

But the old worries and the old guilt and shame soon returned. To my mind I had 'tried Christianity' and it had failed. Thus, I completely ignored the fact that I had left Christ out of the equation—a Christless Christianity?

Nonetheless, when the opportunity to attend the next camp arose a few months later, I couldn't wait to sign up. After all, I reasoned, I can pretend to listen to the God-talk. I was more than ever determined to avoid the 'Christian trap'.

It was good to go back to Belair again and find that a number of the friends I had made at the previous camp had returned. There was just one person to avoid: Miss Cornelius.

Miss Cornelius, one of the camp leaders, was an efficient and daunting senior high-school teacher whom I respected, knowing instinctively that I could never pull the wool over her eyes.

Despite all my plans for keeping a low profile, the following day, Amy Peters, a pretty, fair-haired, quietly spoken girl, cornered me with an awkward question. 'You go to church, don't you, Beth?'

'You could certainly say that,' I answered. 'Four times a Sunday! What do you need to know?'

'I don't know what to think about making a decision for Christ. I only went to church once—when my sister was married.'

'I don't know,' I replied, cautiously. 'Why don't you ask Miss Cornelius?' In suggesting this I felt I'd got myself out of a difficult situation.

However, about an hour later, I was caught out. Miss Cornelius poked her head into the room where I was resting and asked if she might have a word. I could hardly refuse. In she came, sitting herself down beside me and launching straight into her first question.

'What would you think of a salesman who sold goods he didn't believe in, Beth?'

'Not much, Miss Cornelius,' I replied, pretending not to know where she was going with this line of questioning but secretly thinking, *I'll have some fun with you!*

But I had definitely met my match in Miss Cornelius, who began to tell me about the love of Jesus, God's Son, for me. She told me that Christ had taken the punishment for my sins so that I could be forgiven and go free. She didn't have to persuade me that I was a sinner—I knew that only too well. And then came the question I had tried so hard to avoid.

'So, what are you going to do about it, Beth? Will you invite Jesus to be your Saviour?'

There had been so many broken promises and failed relationships in my life I knew instinctively that if Jesus were to fail me my whole life would be destroyed. I couldn't take that chance. To say I was terrified would be putting it mildly. How could I say no to God, but then again, how could I say yes? I was sure God was very angry at me and that this anger must be greater than His love. It was like standing on a huge building so high that the earth below was hidden by swirling clouds and being asked to jump! Around my ears the winds whistled and my body shook with fear. An internal voice was saying, 'Jump… Jesus will catch you!' Yet another voice said, 'But if He doesn't, your life is doomed!' I was paralysed with fear and helpless.

'I am too scared to jump,' I told Miss Cornelius. 'What if there's no-one there to catch me?'

'You remind me of a story about a lad who went hunting for eagles' eggs in the mountains. He walked for some time and saw an eagle fly out from a nest which was in a cave just under the brow of the hilltop. Eagerly he tied his rope to a nearby tree and swung down into the cave, but the rope had been too short. He had to let it go. Landing in the cave, he panicked. He realised that he had a decision to make; the end of the rope would swing back once more near to him. The first time the rope swung back it would be nearest to him and he would be most likely to catch it. However, if he missed it he would fall to his death. On the other hand, if he did not try, he would certainly die in the cave. He took the chance, grabbed the rope, and was saved.'

As she spoke, God lit up this story for me. I believed! I had before me my one opportunity and I jumped. True to His word, Jesus caught me.

I woke up the next morning, smiling. *Something really good happened to me yesterday, and it has changed my life forever.* The joy that came to me then is still with me, more than seventy years later.

The last two days at the camp were strangely comfortable for me. Most of the campers and all of the leaders congratulated me on my decision, and I made friends with a new girl from my class at school. Marie White was a little shorter than my five feet seven inches, with dark, immaculately styled hair and a dusting of light freckles on her nose which she rubbed with her palm when deep in thought.

'Hello Beth. I'm Marie. I've seen you at school… and I've wanted to speak to you. But I'm from the country… and it's such a huge school… and I've been too shy to say anything.'

'I came from a smaller school, too. It's quite scary having fifty-two girls in our class.'

'It's great you decided to follow Jesus. I'm a Christian, too. I go to a church where there's youth group and we have fun times like camp, as well as Bible studies. If you don't go to a church, would you like to come to my church with me?'

'I do go to a church—but it's very different from here: everyone's about a hundred! I'd like to come to church with you, Marie.'

Before we left camp, Marie and I made arrangements to meet again and, as a result, I was much more cheerful about going home.

'What was the camp like?' asked Mum, pushing a mug of cocoa and my favourite snack —a crust of fresh white bread with its lavish coating of dripping—towards me. 'And what's that book in your hand?'

'Camp was fun. And the book is a Bible. Miss Cornelius, one of the leaders, gave it to me.'

'Let me see it,' said Mother, holding out her hand.

Rather reluctantly, I passed over the Bible with its bright blue cover. Miss Cornelius had written in the front of it, and I wasn't sure how my mother would take what she wrote.

Sure enough, she noticed.

'What does this mean: "To Beth, on the occasion of your decision to follow Christ"? I hope you haven't fallen into the clutches of some weird cult!'

'Oh no, Mum. Miss Cornelius's father is a vicar!' I said—with my fingers crossed, bending the truth a little. My Anglican mum wouldn't have been impressed if I'd said 'pastor'. 'She gave me the Bible because I decided to become a Christian at the camp.'

'Become a Christian!' exclaimed my mother. 'Whatever next? You were christened when you were two-and-a-half years old. Will I ever forget it: all dressed in your pretty robe, you were, and when I went to comb your hair you threw a tantrum, backed away from me, and fell backwards into the bath. Your beautiful robe was ruined, so you had to wear an old dress. I was so ashamed. And Uncle Louis was furious because we were late and messed up his first baptismal service. You're certainly a Christian—although sometimes I wonder…'

'Yes, Mum.' I jumped in as my mother paused for effect. 'Will I go and unpack my case now?'

WOULD SUNDAY NEVER COME? Days at home were so dull compared with the lighthearted atmosphere of the camp, but I hadn't even found the courage to ask Mum about going to Marie's church. It would be too awful if she said no.

Mum and I used to go together to a little church at the end of our street, but now that Mum was working she needed to rest on Sunday mornings.

I was still worrying about it when a new idea struck me. I remembered Miss Cornelius' words: 'Don't forget, Beth, you can talk to God about anything that concerns you and He will hear you.'

Perhaps I could pray about this, although it was hard to imagine that God would be interested in whether I went to church when He had so much else to do. But surely it wouldn't hurt to give it a try?

I knelt down by my chair, closed my eyes and prayed. 'Dear God, I want to go to church with Marie on Sunday. Will you help Mum to say yes? Please, God.'

The opportunity came later that day. 'Mum, I want to ask you something. Can I go to Marie's church on Sunday?'

'Well, I suppose that will be all right; Mrs White sounds like a sensible person. Just mind you behave yourself and we'll see.'

I knew that was Mum's way of saying yes and whispered, 'Thank you, God.'

I was up at dawn on Sunday morning so I had

time to have a bath. I put on my best maroon dress with its pleated skirt, grimaced as I pulled on my opaque 60 denier nylon stockings, carefully straightening the seams. Then it was low-heeled court shoes and maroon felt hat—followed by the usual frenetic search for my gloves and handbag.

Twenty minutes riding, most of it uphill, and I arrived safely at the Whites' home in Malvern. I met Marie's parents and we walked ahead of them to the Unley Council Chambers where the service was held.

As we walked, Marie explained that I would probably find the service different from the ones to which I was accustomed; she assured me that it was not a cult.

'Some people call us Plymouth Brethren.'

'How is it different?'

'We don't have a church building and we don't have a paid minister. In the morning service we sit around in a circle and have Communion —but... Here we are; you'll find out more as we go along.'

'Okay.'

I ATTENDED the Brethren Assembly for about three years, until I started my training to be a nurse.

It was the right place for me. The services

were worshipful and reverent, and the Bible studies given by the men of the church were scholarly and spiritually meaningful. My doubts about the divinity of Jesus were answered as the Bible teachers led us through the Old and New Testaments, revealing that the incarnation and life and death of Jesus had been planned for the salvation and freedom of human beings before the world began. All of us have done wrong and all of us need the life Jesus purchased for us by His death. It made sense to me.

Marie was a devout and knowledgeable Christian and Bible student. Before long, she had organised three of us—herself, another girl who had also responded to the Christian message at the camp, and me—as the 'Three Musketeers'. We met regularly, read books—mostly the classics—and studied the Bible together. Another couple at Marie's church ran the young people's group. There were fun-and-games nights, charades, Bible studies and classical music concerts.

Through my new friends, I met and was captivated by the music of such composers as Beethoven, Mozart and Grieg, but the vital change in me was finding God as a loving Father and Jesus as my Saviour, Brother and Friend.

I met Peter and Grace, parents of three children, who kind of adopted me when I was seventeen. Grace became a spiritual mother to me and frequently invited me to their home. Grace, who had developed a remarkable love-relationship with her God, mentored me for years in godly ways of being. There would be joyous days and painful days ahead as I learned, often the hard way, more about ways to treat God and other people. (I am still learning.)

The change affected not only the spiritual and social aspects of my life, but created a new hope that I could succeed if I worked at study.

It's good to celebrate birthdays. I now celebrate two birthdays. I honour and love my earthly parents, grateful for the gift of life they gave me and the sacrifices they made on my behalf. I am also grateful for the new spiritual birth from God.

I AM NOT sure where I first saw it, but a vivid picture has lived in my mind for as long as I can remember: a cloudless blue sky and inviting soft grass—so good to roll in—and two or three joyous lambs, leaping around the feet of the man with the smiling face as he looked down at the little lamb in his arms. I sang my nightly prayer to him, and still do.

> Jesus, tender Shepherd hear me,
>   Bless your little lamb tonight,

> Through the darkness be thou near me,
> Keep me safe 'til morning light.

Today, almost ninety years later, my friend's painting of the same subject, Jesus the Good Shepherd, welcomes me into my bedroom.

Nothing could better describe Jesus' relationship with me in guiding, protecting, loving and forgiving; sadly, I have often been a lamb that wrestled, rather than one that nestled. But that's another tale.

3

FROM SCHOOLGIRL TO NURSE

I had always thought that leaving school would bring only freedom and joy. But when it finally happened, I found it bewildering. My two friends slotted easily into their chosen careers in office work and banking, but neither of these options appealed to me. I had no idea what I wanted to do.

I talked it over with my friends.

'You should pray about it,' advised Marie.

I prayed dutifully. 'Please show me what I should do in the future.'

'Now you need to believe that God will answer your prayer.' Marie reminded me that 'being a Christian means you must learn to trust'.

'How do you think God will answer my prayer?' I queried.

'You will probably be guided by the things that happen to you,' answered Marie.

She was right: I would be guided by my circumstances, but I had a year to wait.

In the meantime, I found a temporary job as a clerk. My employer was a government rehabilitation training scheme for demobilised service personnel. School lessons were posted out, sent for marking and returned to the sender.

It was enjoyable working with six other girls. There were picnics, beach days, parties, and films to watch. There was one hitch. Jolly, auburn-haired Pat arranged a séance with a ouija board. I had no idea what that was, or I wouldn't have attended. (I believe it is dangerous to meddle with unholy spirits.)

But in this instance, just as things became eerie, the lights came back on and the 'spirit' indicated there was one 'discordant' person: me. From the look on Pat's face, she was not impressed.

AT LAST, my waiting time was over for the guiding circumstances to appear.

One day I woke with a persistent pain in my right side. A visit to Dr Messent, who pressed my right side causing me to yelp with pain, resulted in his instant diagnosis.

'You have a grumbling appendix. We'll make an appointment for you to come to hospital and have it removed.'

Two weeks later, propped up on pillows in my white hospital bed, I plied the long-suffering nurses with questions. I decided that—in spite of bedpans and vomit bowls—I wanted above all things to train as a nurse.

Recovering from my appendectomy in record time, I submitted my application to study nursing at the Royal Adelaide Hospital (RAH), and was soon standing with trembling knees at the foot of the staircase leading from Frome Road into the nurses' home, for my interview with Matron Maxwell.

She set me at ease as she clarified the conditions to be met by me if I were to become a probationary nurse. I would work for the first three months without pay. If I proved satisfactory, at the end of that time I would begin my three-year training course. My wage would then be sixteen shillings a week, increasing marginally in my second and third years. If my application was approved, I must purchase two uniform dresses to be worn under the white, starched, hospital-provided aprons. (The pink check regulation uniforms would only be provided once I had successfully passed my probationary period.) I must also provide thick black lisle stockings and black leather shoes. The comical starched white cone-shaped headpiece would be provided.

The hospital would notify me shortly of the result of my application.

I was approved!

After Matron Maxwell retired a few months later someone remarked, 'Wordie, it's lucky that you started training when you did. I've heard that the new matron won't accept aboriginal trainees or any others who are not white.'

As you read my story you will see many 'lucky' or 'coincidental' incidents in my life. While trying to cover up the shame and rejection that I felt when such remarks were made, I murmured my own belief, 'I prayed about it and believe it was God's timing.'

THE FIRST DAY at the RAH was a never to be forgotten experience. Clad in my probationer's uniform, I was introduced to Sister Heneker, a tutor for probationary nurses.

'I will take you to Bice Ward where you will start your training, and introduce you to Sister Dutton.'

As we walked, I recalled the only hospital I knew, the Memorial where my appendix had been removed, and wondered how many three-bed rooms Bice ward contained.

The impressive doors of wood, glass and brass opened to reveal row after row of beds. They weren't just white beds, or even the customary hospital beds. Interspersed between the white were numerous ugly black beds, large wheels one end and spindly legs the other. You could actually see them quiver. I would learn that they were relics from the Crimean War, stored in the hospital basement to be resurrected when the white beds ran out. What a noise they made as they thundered and thumped their way through the echoing corridors.

I soon adjusted to the normal 'broken shifts' with their 6 am starts and 8 pm finishes. During breaks from 10 am to 12 noon and 4 pm to 6 pm, we returned to the wards to help with meals. We might also be needed to work after 8 pm to make dressings, rolling swabs and spreading cod liver oil on the dressings we had made.

On the afternoon when we worked straight through (normally before our weekly day off), we made the evening meals for the patients. What a rush! Hurrying through the ward with pen and paper, demanding breathlessly from each patient, 'What will you have for tea? Salad, sandwich, or scrambled egg?'

We would have to prepare food for perhaps thirty patients in a large ward, deliver it, then collect the dishes so that the ward staff could wash the dishes, clean the kitchen and go off-duty on time. The bread was fresh, warm and… so hard to slice while the fretful voice of the wardsmen intoned, 'You'd better hurry, nurse. I pull the plugs out of the sink at 5 pm.'

Beth at the nurses' quarters at Royal Adelaide Hospital

As the very new recruits, we were expected to perform the more revolting tasks, but recoiled when first faced with a gigantic trough and its floating collection of battered, odoriferous bed pans to be scrubbed. Another memory remains of sweeping the vast floor of the ward with a sore arm following injections for typhoid or other diseases.

But in wondrous contrast to these experiences was the real camaraderie and joy with our fellow nurses, plus the challenge of learning new skills. Many of us would still say these ranked among the happiest days of our lives.

Bice was a women's medical ward. I was incredulous when I learned that some patients were nursed on the open balcony, protected by stiff canvas blinds attached with metal fittings. Cold air streamed through the gaps as the blinds flapped.

Some of these patients suffered from tuberculosis while others had been paralysed during the infantile paralysis epidemic years before, and relied on noisy 'iron lungs' to promote their breathing. It was heart-wrenching to observe the conditions that kept these people in a sort of semi-existence. Their bravery amazed and humbled me.

I had been waiting expectantly for the next step of my nursing career—taking temperatures. There was an element of fear in the process.

Every nurse who broke a thermometer must present herself to matron and account for the tragedy. One day it happened—what I had most feared. I picked up a thermometer and I swear to you as I later swore to matron, that although I wiped it SO gently, the end just fell off.

Crossing the quadrangle with reluctant feet, I sat alone in the barren corridor outside the office, polishing my black shoes on my black stockings and practising my speech, until the summons came to confess my crime.

'Well, Matron, it was like this: as I wiped it the top fell off. I'm very sorry.'

'I hope you'll be more careful next time, nurse.'

I was—very careful, and never needed to repeat the performance.

The discovery and use of penicillin had revolutionised nursing procedures. Senior nurses looked at us with envy, telling how they used to cry when a patient was admitted with pneumonia. In the days prior to antibiotics, the disease would progress to the point of crisis, after which the patient would either die or recover. Patients needed intense, exhausting care; mere injections seemed too easy. Our nursing predecessors believed the quality of nursing would suffer.

The patients weren't so sure about the blessings of antibiotics when they were injected three or four times a day. I couldn't recommend our syringes or needles for their condition or their sterility, but they had certainly been well used! Each morning, the sterile syringes and needles would be placed in a large flat dish and covered with antiseptic. For a large ward there might be a dozen of each. When they were required, they would be lifted out with forceps, used, rinsed, and returned to the antiseptic until required again, without further sterilisation.

Night duty was a new experience for me. We were rostered for several weeks working from 10 pm, with one night off per week. My first experience was in Light Ward, a men's ward, intended for about forty patients but always overcrowded and housing up to seventy patients. There were many of the black, wheeled beds.

The wards assumed a rather eerie, shadowy atmosphere at night, but the sound effects produced by so many men needed to be heard to be believed: snores, whistles, groans and crashes, blended with the threatening THUMP-CLUMP-rattle of one more black iron bedstead arriving from the basement.

Some patients were disoriented and tried to get out of bed. One man cut the cords of the heavy weights attached to his legs with thunderous effect. There were beds surrounded by heavy wooden screens from which came the sounds of rattling arrhythmic breathing, worrying silences, followed by tremendous gulps of air, great gulps, gradually growing weaker. You knew that person was not going to live very long, but there was insufficient room for the care needed and the dignity due.

The RAH was the only public hospital.

ONE OF THE great benefits of my nursing career was the association with the other nurses. I was particularly blessed to have begun my training with Helen Albrecht, whose parents were missionaries on Hermannsburg Mission in the Northern Territory, serving our First Nations people.

We would remain close friends for almost seventy years until Helen passed away. As friends we prayed, studied, rode horses and enjoyed life together. Her untiring works for others were rewarded by a richly deserved Medal of the Order of Australia.

Another colleague, Mary, was almost forty when she began her nursing career. Kind, energetic and full of good advice, she took me under her wing. When we realised that the dates of our holidays coincided, she invited me to spend them with her at Port Pirie, a mining town north of Adelaide.

Mary had a younger brother, a quiet gentle man whom I instinctively liked. He showed me the sights of Port Pirie and we had long, serious discussions about God. He had never given much thought to 'religion', but found that there was a gap in his life. Before very long, he was making a decision that Christ, the Son of God was the Person he wanted to follow for the rest of his life.

As we spent time together, he fell in love with me and I fell in love with being loved. I revelled in the unaccustomed attention, in being protected and showered with gifts. But when my friend talked of marriage, I realised how selfish I had been. I had never been 'in love', and already believed that I would go to Africa as a missionary.

My friend was very sad, but the story has a happy ending. Mary's best friend had been in love with him for years. I happened to bump into them a year later on their honeymoon; they were radiant.

ON MY RETURN from holidays to begin my second-year training, I was surprised to see that my name was down for a share-room with a Fiona McDonald. This was most unusual. The nurses' home was crowded, and we frequently shared with six or more other nurses. Still fearful of new relationships and not knowing Fiona, I wondered what she would be like.

I found the room, unpacked and waited nervously for my new roommate to appear. The door opened and my anxiety surfaced, for Fiona was tall, slim and elegant. She moved gracefully, her voice was beautifully modulated, her glossy brown hair curled naturally, and her deep blue eyes sparkled. She radiated confidence and subtle perfume: a perfect picture of the person I would like to have been. I, however, was untidy and insecure, lacking any sense of identity, a person who tested the environment in order to conform. I knew instinctively that our relationship was doomed.

'Hello,' lilted my roommate. 'I'm Fiona, but everyone calls me Fee.'

'Hello Fee, I'm Elizabeth, but everyone calls me Beth.'

We both laughed.

'It'll be great rooming with just one other person instead of six, don't you think?' queried Fee with a friendly smile.

'Yeah, it means ten minutes longer in bed when we don't need to fight for the bathroom.'

As the months passed, Fee's sunny disposition and positive outlook affected my life. Rather than viewing my racial heritage as a disadvantage, she found it intriguing.

'I shall call you Elizabeth,' she stated firmly, 'and you will be my Island Princess.'

We both laughed, knowing it was not true, but nonetheless I found it oddly comforting. For once I had the impression that I was not looking up to a superior person but to one with whom I was an equal and a true friend.

When our days off coincided, I would go with her to her beautiful home at Waterfall Gully where we would go horse-riding over the hills, Fee on her glossy chestnut pony, and I atop an aristocratic white Arab steed. He was previously a circus horse, though he loved to prance with proudly arched neck and flowing mane while I, acutely conscious of the incongruity, practised my best 'sack of potatoes' routine in the saddle.

We talked a lot, too, and I learned that Fee was in love with a handsome squadron leader in the Royal Australian Air Force who seemed a little reluctant to pop the question. 'But I'm going to Sydney to see him in exactly six months from now and I can hardly wait—perhaps THIS time I'll come back engaged.'

'I'm sure you will, Fee,' I soothed.

'Have you ever been in love, Beth?' queried Fee.

'Not really. I thought I was for a while, until he proposed.'

'What happened then?'

'I was terrified because he really loved me,

but I wasn't in love with him. And I think I will be working overseas when I finish my training.'

'Tell me more.'

'Well, when I was sixteen, I gave my life to God, and since then I think He wants me to work in Africa.'

Fee and I talked together many times. She was most interested when I told her how my life had been completely changed by my faith in Jesus. One day, a few months later, she confided that she had just made the same decision. Believing that Jesus Christ, the Son of God, had given His life for her, she had asked forgiveness for her sins and given her life to Him.

I could see that my friend had found joy and peace in her new relationship with God, but one thing troubled her greatly: she had not told John, the man she loved.

Time passed quickly. It was early Saturday morning, and she was to leave for Sydney that afternoon to meet her beloved John.

'He has always known that I was an atheist,' she wailed. 'Whatever will he do now I am a Christian? It might mean the end of everything.'

I shared Fee's concern, and as I prayed for them the thought came of a tract by Robert A. Laidlaw, *Finding the Way*, that set out the Christian way more clearly than anything else I knew. If only I could get a copy in time for Fee to take it with her, that afternoon, it would give John the perfect explanation for the change in his girlfriend's life. However, I was working in theatre until 5 pm and the Christian bookshop shut at midday. It was impossible. What a pity.

At midday, I was cleaning in the back room adjacent to the theatre when a Christian medical student (Harold Steward, who afterwards became a well-known Adelaide GP) walked in. For some unknown reason, he began emptying his pockets onto a table nearby, and to my amazement, the familiar yellow-covered tract *Finding the Way* appeared.

'Harold, do you need that tract?'

'No, Beth. I just had the urge from God to put it in my pocket this morning. Do you need it?'

'Yes please.'

At lunchtime, I rushed to the nurses' home and gave it to Fee.

I was off-duty the day Fee arrived back in Adelaide, but when I caught up with her the next day her usual brightness was heightened by a new radiance.

'Congratulations, Fee. I can tell by your face John popped the question at last!'

'Yes, but that's only half of it. I tried to talk to John, but I just couldn't explain. When it was time to leave, he still hadn't proposed, but I left him *Finding the Way* and you'll never guess!'

'So, tell me quickly!'

'He rang, told me how much he loved me and asked me to marry him.'

'What did you say?'

'As if you don't know—I said yes really fast. After a while he said he had something else important to tell me; the fact I was an atheist stopped him from proposing earlier because, although he hadn't thought much about religion himself, he didn't want his children to be brought up by an atheist. But best of all, after he read *Finding the Way* he made a decision to follow Jesus. I felt happier about that than I did about being engaged. Will you be my bridesmaid?'

'Of course!'

Fee never completed her nursing course. A few months later she and John were married at St Matthew's Church, Kensington and I had the joy of being her bridesmaid. They joined the diplomatic service and worked in Europe.

At seventeen or eighteen, in my day we were much younger than the worldly-wise seventeen- or eighteen-year-olds of today. I had been sheltered to some extent, compared to some of the people I met. We are concerned about the depressed teenagers of the 2020s, but the same situation was apparent following World War II. One older nurse whom I knew well just walked out into the sea. I had no idea of the extent of her loneliness. I received testimonies from two other, younger nurses who were miraculously rescued at the last moment.

Another nurse, Mary, had been depressed for most of her life. She had suffered a birth injury which scarred her face. Her family life had been traumatic, and she had been planning suicide for some time.

She bought a ticket on the boat that sailed from Adelaide to Kangaroo Island—she liked boat trips—and planned that when they reached midstream she would find some way of slipping over the rail. She walked towards the railing, but a passenger appeared, so she sat down. She noticed a paper that had been blown against the seat, so she picked it up and began reading.

It was a copy of the Salvation Army paper *The War Cry*. She was quite fascinated. She read there about a Jesus she had never known. Her heart was deeply touched, and she postponed her suicide forever. She later married and lived a happy life. I can see her now, dear Mary. She said, 'The paper was just caught. There it was and I read it.'

Another friend, Elaine, had done most of her training in the UK.

She told me about her experience of being deeply wounded and terribly depressed as a young person. She came from a wealthy family, greatly respected in Australia. Not wanting to disgrace her relatives, Elaine decided she'd go to

England and there commit suicide. She booked into a boarding house, amassed numerous sleeping tablets and on the chosen day she composed herself, lay down, and swallowed the lot.

Just as she swallowed the last capsule, there was a knock at the door. A young woman poked her head into the room saying, 'I'm a Christian and I believe God wants us to talk. I haven't got the time now. Could I meet you at lunchtime?'

My friend answered, 'Yes, if I'm able to I will.' She couldn't understand why the tablets had no effect on her, but the Christian girl came back at lunchtime. Elaine found peace in Christ.

OUR THREE-YEAR COURSE ended with exams, written and spoken. I had never worked at study and my school results had been less than impressive. I was scared and so was my mum, who aimed to bribe me.

'If you get a credit in your exams, I'll give you ten pounds,' she promised.

Intending to make a joke, I answered, 'What will you give me if I top the state?'

'Forty pounds,' she promised.

My exam was astonishing—I was asked everything I had learned. You should have seen Mum's face when I said, 'You owe me forty pounds.'

Miss Powell, who had been my first-year high-school teacher, was apparently leafing through *The Advertiser* newspaper and came across the state nursing exam results for 1947. She was so surprised to see that I had topped the state in my nursing exams that she wrote me a letter.

'Elizabeth, I want to congratulate you on your success in gaining top marks in the South Australian nursing examinations. Whatever happened to you?'

Beth Wordie, Registered Nurse

My answer was insufferably pious and preachy—but the truth.

'You ask what has happened to me—four years ago I discovered God's love for me in Jesus Christ and gave my life to Jesus. Since then, God has been transforming my life and I know this success is due to God.'

Although most people who finished training when I did were asked to work at the hospital, I was not asked. I couldn't have accepted anyway—I was going straight to Melbourne to study midwifery.

4

CALL THE MIDWIFE

My twenty-first birthday was fast approaching. I loved parties and was determined to celebrate. I sent invitations to my six best nursing friends, bought the food, decorated our lounge room, and prepared a selection of games and quizzes. We all enjoyed ourselves.

My time at the Royal Adelaide Hospital would soon be over. I had made plans to study midwifery at the Queen Victoria Hospital in Melbourne. An Adelaide girl born and bred, I had never travelled further than Mount Gambier. I had no acquaintances in Victoria and knew of no-one else who would be studying at the Queen Vic. My mood vacillated between excitement and trepidation.

On the morning of my departure, I had no

need of the shrilling of an alarm clock. The disordered bed bore witness to my restless night. Two things gave me confidence: the amount of time I had spent in prayer, and my impeccable preparation for the day.

My cases were packed, including the classy brown hat case that was the pride of my life, and whose battered remains are still with me. My mother and I had decided to say our goodbyes at home: finances were at ebb tide. I would catch a tram to Adelaide Station.

There was a certain element of the smug as I reviewed the perfection of my plans; I was usually known for leaving all until the last moment. Part of my plan was to leave home two hours before the Melbourne Express pulled out, which was just as well. When I arrived at the station, more than an hour early, I discovered I had left my ticket at home. A mad dash in a taxi brought me back to the barrier, breathless and agitated, just in time.

Being accustomed to the motley collection of buildings which made up the Royal Adelaide Hospital, I was impressed by the substantial orderly buildings of the Queen Victoria Women's Hospital on the corner of Swanston and Lonsdale Streets, Melbourne. It was even more impressive to learn that the forerunner of this hospital which opened in 1893 was at that time one of three hospitals worldwide dedicated solely to the care of women by women, and which offered training for women doctors. What vision it must have required of the many women who flocked to donate to the Shilling Fund.

The decision to employ only women doctors had its consequences for us. On the rare occasions when massive strength was required for a forceps delivery, it was customary to call for the services of a very strong, muscular woman surgeon. On night duty I once espied her, striding through the ward in her colourfully striped silk pyjamas. She was never known to fail.

As an only child, I had little knowledge of pregnancy and childbirth, and looked forward to learning more. Soon after the course commenced, the new recruits attended the prenatal clinic. A lecture illustrated with vivid charts was followed by my introduction to a heavily pregnant mum who had graciously volunteered to an external examination.

First, find the baby's heartbeat. I adjusted the stethoscope, moved it over the swollen stomach, and listened. I soon heard a clear steady heartbeat. I moved the stethoscope, and was sure, well almost sure, there was a second heartbeat.

'Well,' enquired Sister, 'what did you find, Nurse?'

'I th-think she has twins. I heard two heartbeats, Sister.'

The patient took a deep, anxious breath and

Sister, with a disapproving frown at me, hastened to assure her. 'This was Nurse's first examination. I can assure you there is only one baby.'

However, as you may have guessed, learner's luck was with me. There were indeed twins. Sister couldn't resist a little sarcastic hollow homage, pretending to call me for consultation when there was a problem. I soon regretted my situation.

Surely no midwife will ever forget their first delivery and I will never forget Gwen Thomas. Under ordinary circumstances she would have been a slim, quietly-spoken young woman with an attractive smile but now, in labour with her first baby, she was fearful. In those days the husband was banished, and I would be her companion for the next few hours. Between contractions we discussed many things, among them, Christian names. I told her my name was Elizabeth, something which was forbidden as a professional.

The labour proceeded normally through its stages and Mrs Thomas used the gas as she needed. The baby's head emerged, and a beautiful, perfect baby girl made her appearance, but Mrs Thomas, groggy from the anaesthetic, was slow to respond to the supervising doctor's demands for her to look at the baby. Her bleary eyes circled the scene until they came to me. A beatific smile encompassed her face as she whispered, 'Elizabeth, I knew you'd be here!'

Sister was not amused.

'Do you know this patient, Nurse?' she demanded.

'No, Sister.'

'Then I will talk to you later, Nurse.'

And she did!

I very much enjoyed my nine months at the Queen Victoria Hospital, delivering the quota of babies allotted to me. I visited private homes as in the television show *Call the Midwife* except I travelled to my clients via Melbourne trams, not a bike.

My decision to study midwifery was in line with my intention to work in Africa in areas where there would be no medical help, but the first emergency call came when I went home to Adelaide.

I was reminded of this recently. In 2020, shortly after I had moved to the nursing home, daydreaming in a supermarket queue, I was startled when a voice behind me rang out, 'You were Beth Wordie, and you saved my life.'

I turned to see a middle-aged woman whom I didn't recognise at first.

'I was Jacqui Francis. Do you remember me?'

'I could never forget you, Jacqui,' I answered. We talked for a while, planned to meet again and

I returned home, sat down with a cup of tea, put my feet up and relived the past.

It was March 1952, and my good friend Noel Francis was in the last stages of her third pregnancy when she rang me with a request.

'I feel anxious about the birth of this baby and my mum is no longer around to come to hospital with me. Would you come?'

'I'd love to. Thanks for asking me.'

It seemed that Noel would be on time with the birth, and I went to stay with the family a few days prior to the expected date.

About five o'clock one evening the contractions began. Noel's husband, Brian, wasted no time in getting the car out. I decided to wear a white uniform to look inconspicuous, and we were on our way. Noel's previous labours had been short, which gave more anxiety to the situation.

We pulled up at the doors of the maternity section of Memorial Hospital. Brian turned the car around and returned home to care for the two older children.

As the duty sister pulled out a chart and began to take Noel's details, the phone rang with an urgent summons for her to go to the upstairs labour ward where a patient was haemorrhaging. There were two labour wards—one upstairs and the other downstairs.

Noel and I were left alone in the office, and

Noel's contractions were increasing in number and strength. We were afraid. I went looking to find someone or the ground floor labour theatre. I found the theatre, examined a young woman who was in labour, questioned her and felt her stomach. It was her first baby, and she had a long way to go before delivery. So she led me back to her room and I put her to bed, then ran back to Noel and installed her into the labour room. I ran upstairs to where the doctor had just finished with the emergency there, and half-dragged him away. As we entered the labour room, Noel was about to deliver. To our horror, the doctor and I saw the plump white umbilical cord wrapped three times around Jacqui's throat.

With quick dexterity, the surgeon grabbed the scissors and cut the cord just in time.

Looking back, Noel's courage and faith and co-operation amazed me. But how did I know what to do in a strange hospital? There was no time to spare.

Why had I worn a white uniform just to sit with a patient? It would have been far more difficult had I not appeared to have authority.

I believe God guided us. I give Him the glory while feeling privileged to be of service.

Two aspects will always remain with me: the miracle of birth itself and the cruelty of our tendency to judge before we know the circumstances. The first aspect, the miracle of childbirth, is apparent. The second was demonstrated by the situation of a patient whom I will call Mrs Bailey.

The nursing staff were notified that Mrs Bailey was on her way to the ward. She was described as a lady in her late thirties who had procured an abortion but now had a life-threatening infection, gas gangrene. Mrs Bailey looked older than her stated age, her eyes were swollen from sobbing, and it was a few days later that I was given the privilege of hearing her story as she spoke through her tears.

'I believe in God and I love my church. I never wanted to abort my baby, but I was desperate. I already have six children and we live in a tiny hut on the wharves. My husband doesn't have regular work and the children we have now are not fed and cared for properly. What else could I do?'

The question hung between us. What would I have done? I had no answer except to believe that our loving Father would forgive the repentant and look after both mother and unborn child.

5

PREPARATION FOR AFRICA

I was sixteen when I first felt God's call on my life. I kept saying to the Lord, 'Shut the door if you don't want me to do this.' By 1951, my preparation had included three years of nursing and one of midwifery.

My next tasks were to study for two years at a Bible college, and to visit church congregations and other groups informing them of the work of the Sudan Interior Mission in Africa, giving them the opportunity to support me on the mission field.

Because I would be going overseas for four years, leaving my mother alone, I decided to study at Adelaide Bible Institute. I would not be living with my mother during this time, but I could visit her regularly, and keep an eye on her health and wellbeing.

SIM was an independent and interdenominational 'faith mission'. It provided mission stations in Africa, but individual missionaries weren't guaranteed a wage. We were expected to provide for our own needs, including household equipment.

My mother gasped when she saw the list for the first time.

'How can you possibly afford all those things? Where's the money coming from? Even after all that studying, you've never ever earned a good wage. How will you manage to pay for them?'

'Well, Mum, if it's God's plan for me to go to Africa, God will sort out the problems. If it's just my idea, I don't want to go anyway. We'll wait and see what happens.'

We did wait and we did see—as goods flooded in—that God could choose someone as weak and faulty as me to go to Sudan, as a missionary nurse. The ability to collect all these essentials was seen as one of the indications that God had called me to the SIM.

What a time I had, in the weeks leading up to my departure, amassing all the things needed to set up house in 'darkest Africa': tables, chairs, saucepans, brooms, cutlery, crockery, clothing, sheets, pillows and, finally, enough toilet paper for four years!

In the end there was a total of twenty-eight

boxes, barrels and crates to be loaded aboard the liner for a voyage that would take several weeks.

THERE IS something about living with constant noise. It irritates you at first and you can't sleep. Later on, it wakes you up when it stops. At least, that is what happened to me.

Silence at last! I said to myself. *It must be Aden. Time to leave the boat.*

One last wave to Richard and June as I disembarked. I was relieved to see my twenty-eight boxes and barrels had been safely unloaded onto the flat-bottomed barge bobbing around metres below the deck of the liner.

Finally, at the age of twenty-eight, I was in Aden at the western end of the Arabian Peninsula, waiting to begin my life in Sudan beyond the Red Sea. Preparing for my life as a missionary nurse in tribal areas would involve a preliminary period in Khartoum, the capital city of Anglo-Egyptian Sudan, located where the Blue Nile meets the White Nile. I would be in Khartoum for three months, becoming acclimatised and studying Arabic, the trade language of Sudan.

As the plane took off from Aden, skirting the Red Sea, I reflected on the path my life had taken.

Life had really started for me when, as a confused and fearful sixteen-year-old, I had discovered that God really loved me, and I had given my life to God. My friend Dorothy often quoted these words from the Bible: 'God has given us a future and a hope.' That's just what God had done for me and I thanked Him.

I was half asleep when the anxious sound of throttled-back engines alerted me that we were approaching Khartoum.

The heat of the tarmac burnt through my shoes as I walked to the airport lounge. The sun scorched the top of my head, and I now understood the value of the infamous pith helmet! My eyes watered and I squinted at the glare of sun on glass and white shirts.

I was met by Enid Forsberg, whose reassuring, kindly face put me at ease. Once we had collected my suitcase, we were soon on the road leading to the city. My twenty-eight boxes and barrels would arrive at SIM headquarters later, by rail.

'Well Beth, it looks as if Khartoum has prepared a welcome for you,' said Enid.

'I'm not sure what you mean,' I replied.

'Just look at the road ahead—do you see that brown cloud?'

I looked, and saw that the road ahead was obscured by a billowing mass racing towards us at breakneck speed.

'That's a dust storm. The name for them here

is "haboob". We will have to pull over and wait. Quickly! Wind up your window!'

Enid turned on the lights and pulled over onto the verge as she spoke, but we were already engulfed in complete darkness. A mighty wind grasped the car and shook it mercilessly. Stones and gravel hurled themselves against the roof and sides of the car, deafening us. It was hard to breathe. Fine dust whirled around us, seeping in through the tiniest spaces.

After what seemed a very long time—but was probably no more than half an hour—the noise lessened, and the car stopped rocking. A little light returned, and, after a few protesting hiccups, the haboob departed—and the day returned to normal.

SIM HEADQUARTERS WAS an impressive two-storey building. I thought it was brick to begin with, but it was simulated brick cladding.

The main focus of the mission was not in Khartoum, but in the countryside, five hundred miles south of Khartoum. There were a number of individual mission stations each working with a different tribe of people: the Dinka, Uduk, Hill Baruun, Mabaan. Each tribe spoke in its own language that rarely resembled those of its neighbouring tribes. Communication between tribal groups was possible through the use of basic Arabic.

On a typical station there would be four or five foreign missionaries who were involved in evangelism, translation of the Scriptures, and schooling for the children; or nursing in the medical clinic staffed by a nurse and local tribespeople.

The SIM plan for me involved first learning some Arabic in Khartoum before beginning work in Chali el Fil with the Uduk people.

THE CITY of Khartoum delighted me—it was so different from anything I had ever experienced. Established as an army camp in 1829, it had been the scene of wars, insurrections, massacres, riots, sieges, epidemics, famines and flooding. It had been occupied by both the Egyptians and the British.

Geographically, the city is located at the confluence of the Blue Nile—which rises in Ethiopia, cascading through deep gorges, picking up little silt so that its waters retain a clear bluish tint; and the White Nile—which meanders through flatter countryside via Uganda gathering silt, and arriving in Khartoum cloudy and whitish. The waters mingle and flow together to form the mighty Nile that flows north through Egypt to the Mediterranean.

Khartoum was a cosmopolitan city in 1954. There were parties hosted by local Greek families and I experienced a gigantic Greek wedding. They commiserated with me because I wasn't married, saying, 'Next year, it will be you.'

I met Sam and Mary Helen Burns at the missionary home. They were in Khartoum for Mary Helen to be tested because of this wonderful thing: a first pregnancy in her forties. Sam had been in the English army and Mary Helen a missionary from the United States. Sam made the mistake of taking me—a person of mixed heritage—to the British Club. I actually went for a swim in the pool at the club. I think he was taken aside and told off. He never told me what happened—but I was never invited to the British Club again.

THE STREETS ABOUNDED WITH LIFE. It seemed to me that, at home in Australia, the streets are like corridors through which we hurry to reach our destination with heads down, noticing very little. In central Khartoum, however, the streets were very much a part of life: loud music, different exotic and highly-spiced smells from wonderful pancake meals, men with their white jubbas and turbans, women with multi-coloured robes and semi-veiled faces. The vibrant streets and clothes hid a lot of things. They practised the Pharaonic style—the most radical form—of female circumcision. A lot of things were hidden under the festive surface.

It was a very attractive city in lots of other ways, too. I was startled by the demented braying of the donkeys, with their long ears and big brown eyes and determined waywardness, and the huffings of the camels with their padding feet and their supercilious way of looking down their long bottom lips. Their extraordinarily long eyelashes—mainly to keep the sand out of their eyes in the desert—added to their mystique. Even bull camels have the most fetching eyelashes.

Khartoum is really a not-very-old city. It had been set up as a sort of English army camp and in a patriotic way they had laid it out like the British flag—which meant that it wasn't very good for traffic. The streets connected at sharp angles all over the place. I heard the local fatalistic belief—if it's your day to get killed you can't stay alive and if it's your day to stay alive, you can't get killed. This seemed to make a lot of difference to the way drivers approached travelling on the road—it was a form of blatant attack rather than a respectful 'live and let live'.

Travelling anywhere was accompanied by a cacophony of noise and movement—incessant honking of horns and grinding of brakes as vehicles came to sudden stops. Cars rushed by, narrowly avoiding casual pedestrians. Animals competed with the cars for road space. Elegantly haughty camels with ornate trappings vied with overladen donkeys that retaliated with startling snorts and vicious hooves. At times you would see poor creatures with broken legs, abandoned to die on the road where they had fallen under their immense loads.

Carol—a new arrival to the mission from the USA—and I once carried water to an animal left dying in the heat. I have since wondered whether we did the right thing or whether we just prolonged its agony, but the relief in the creature's tortured face impelled us to continue our mercy mission.

Strident summons to prayer from the muezzin clashed with tantalisingly unfamiliar music erupting from the cafes, and anyone who has never tasted kissra and mullah is to be greatly pitied. To think of them activates my sluggish taste buds and initiates a saliva flow that is bound to die unsatiated except in my dreams. Mullah is the most fragrant stew you can imagine: meat and vegetables, embraced, cuddled, lovingly stewed in a savoury potpourri of Sudanese spices; it is unlike anything else I have ever sampled. The only possible accompaniment worthy of such excellence is kissra. Finely ground dura grain is soaked in water until it thickens and assumes a delicately fermented flavour. It is then spread onto an oiled sheet of iron—approximately fifty by forty centimetres—and cooked for a short time over a hot fire. The result is a large, very thin but succulent sheet that is parcelled up and dipped into the mullah. To be in a place where kissra and mullah are created is to be blessed by an olfactory experience without parallel!

THE CITY of Khartoum was naturally divided into three by its location at the confluence of the Blue and White Niles; Europeans like us often lived in Khartoum number one. For my lessons in Arabic, I needed to cross a bridge over the Nile to get to my teacher's residence in Khartoum number two.

I wanted to learn Arabic. It is a gorgeous language. Some of its sounds are very smooth and seductive; others, especially if spoken in anger, can sound as if you are clearing your throat to spit.

In a country like the Sudan where there may be hundreds of tribal languages, it is essential to have one common language, a 'trade language' to enable communication throughout. Arabic was that language in the Sudan, and I would need it in my clinic.

I had only been in Khartoum a few days when it was time for my first lesson. I would go alone to Sheik Sadiq's home. It would be necessary for me to hail a 'tarha'—an ordinary car where the driver shouted his destination, for example 'Omdurman!' or 'Khartoum nimera wahid!' and so on, and pick up a carful of passengers who responded. This car would drop me at the right place and after my lesson in Arabic writing, the sheik would direct me to my lady language teacher, Sitt Faith, who would then take me to a bus to bring me home. It sounded simple, and I don't want to boast, but it is almost routine for me to get lost.

It's not my fault! If the first school I attended had not forcibly changed me from being strongly left-handed to being weakly right-handed I would have been a normal human being. As it is, my brain is muddled. Fortunately, I had broken a bottle and had a scar on my right thumb, so I knew right.

My first lesson with the sheik was over. He called his twelve-year-old son, and gave him instructions, in Arabic, to get me to Sitt Faith's home. The boy nodded and we set off.

The streets were quite dark in this particular area of Khartoum Number Two; families lived behind high walls and high closed gates. Women were to be veiled outside the home. I padded along behind the sheik's son for a quarter of an hour.

Suddenly, the boy stopped in front of a high gate and knocked. The cover over the tiny eye-hole at the top of the gate was pulled back, an eye appeared for an instant and the cover quickly closed. We waited outside, or at least I waited—the sheik's lad had vanished without a trace. I was lost, alone and speechless.

The high gate opened slowly and a burly gatekeeper beckoned me in. What a contrast to the dusty street: soft green lawn, attractive bushes and a flowing fountain. Six people, three men and three women, rose from the lounges on which they had been resting.

Chairs were brought, smiles and courteous gestures invited me to sit and partake of the soft drinks and sweets that suddenly appeared. We sat and smiled and looked at each other. My previous fearful visions of possible newspaper headlines—'Adelaide woman disappears in Khartoum'—faded as I lisped 'Sitt Faith', 'Sheik Sadiq', and 'Australia', as one does. Blank stares rewarded my efforts.

Suddenly, one of the men had an idea. A discussion in fluent Arabic was followed by his disappearance into the street, which in turn was followed by the reassuring purr of a costly limousine, out of which emerged the man who had left, followed by another extremely handsome man who greeted me in flawless English. I would later learn that he was a well-known army colonel.

Very soon, enthroned in the lavish comfort of the limo, I was assuring the attentive colonel that I MUST catch the bus. Thank you, but I couldn't visit his wives. He dropped me at the bus, but followed it for several stops, imploring me to come with him to see his home.

My mission was shocked. Sheik Sadiq exploded. In their eyes, the scandal would rock Khartoum. And it was somehow my fault.

I didn't mind at all. It was a real adventure and I had thoroughly enjoyed it. But I was never trusted to go to other classes. They came to me. Ah well!

The Mahdi's tomb, looking across the Nile from Khartoum

A donkey loaded with grass

The train station in Khartoum

6

FROM KHARTOUM TO CHALI EL FIL

My heart was light as I turned to take a last look at the mission house in Khartoum from the back seat of the car that was taking another missionary, Grace, and me to the airport. Although I'd had been very happy studying Arabic for the past three months in Khartoum, I was impatient now to begin the work for which I had spent so long in preparation: bringing medical help to tribal peoples in outback areas of Sudan.

I was marvelling at the patience of God and singing under my breath, 'To God be the glory, great things He has done,' as we entered the gate to the aerodrome. On the tarmac I could see a small, antiquated biplane, panting asthmatically. As we approached, a tall, fair-haired man emerged from the cockpit, wiping his hands on an oily cloth, and calling out to us in a cheerful voice with a heavy Dutch accent.

'Good morning. My name is Hank. We have a good day for flying, thank God.'

'Good morning to you, too, Hank,' replied Enid, who had driven us from Khartoum. 'You already know Grace. This is Beth—she is going up-country for the first time.'

After our brief farewells and thanks to Enid, Grace and I occupied two seats behind Hank—in an area not much larger than a car. Once we were settled, the bulky plane waddled down the runway, picked up speed, and took off, soaring like a bird once it was loosed into its natural element.

The engine noise was too loud to allow easy conversation, so we watched silently as the country rolled under us. The terrain reminded me of Australia: areas of stark, stony desert, interspersed with relatively flat green areas with scattered trees; but there were differences: the shiny ribbons indicating the Blue and White Niles, and between them the Gezira—a green cultivated island that utilised the gradient between the two rivers to provide natural, free irrigation.

The only excitement during the flight: when Hank needed to switch over to another tank of fuel, he decided to give us a thrill by allowing a short time to elapse between switching tanks. The plane's sudden drop was surprising, and I think Hank was a little disappointed—both Grace and I passed the test with 'flying' colours!

I travelled the major part of the journey from Khartoum to Chali el Fil in the plane. The remainder of the journey—several hundred miles—would be completed by jeep.

It was good to come to the end of the rather monotonous plane ride and to feel solid ground beneath my feet. Pete, who was in charge of the mission station, welcomed us and introduced us to Chuck, a lanky, laid-back Texan, who was to drive me many jolting miles to the mission at Chali el Fil the following day.

That evening, we were having 'supper', as the Americans called it, when suddenly, through the window, we saw the flash of burning torches and heard loud voices.

Pete pushed back his chair from the table and went quickly to the door. After a short conversation in a very strange-sounding language, he returned, saying, 'Beth, some men have brought in a young girl who is in strong labour—please come quickly.'

I rose from the table and went quickly outside to be confronted by the saddest sight I had ever witnessed. Six dark African men, holding spears, semi-naked with tribal skin markings glowing white in the torchlight, gathered around a girl who lay on the ground, groaning in pain. I guessed she could be about fourteen years old.

Her grossly swollen stomach indicated that she was in the late stages of pregnancy. Her eyes were filled with tears and she whimpered as her stomach tightened with another contraction.

A sinister figure, clad in a leopard skin, iridescent black feathers in his hair, face and body streaked with garish white ashes, muttered incantations as he slashed the throat of a terrified rooster.

I knelt down and examined the girl, speaking quietly to her, and gently touching her distended stomach.

There was nothing I could do. She was a small girl with a large baby. There was no doctor, no clinic, and no medicine within a hundred miles.

We watched with breaking hearts as the forlorn group disappeared into the darkness.

THE DRIVE next day to the mission at Chali seemed endless. The terrain—green, pleasant and undulating—became monotonous after the first few hours. The deeply rutted roadway shook and rattled the jeep until my aching bones begged for mercy.

At last, the jeep slowed. We turned into the mission compound. I had wondered what our accommodation would be like and was happy to see three red-brick mission houses, a small brick medical clinic, and a 'church' building—grass-roofed, low sides, and row upon row of the narrowest of slatted benches.

Three women stood outside the third building, waiting to greet us. As Chuck and I stumbled from the vehicle, stretching our weary limbs, the tallest of the women stepped forward with outstretched hands to welcome us.

'Hi Chuck, good to see you. And welcome to Chali, Beth.' She spoke in a voice that revealed her origins in America's south. 'I am Mary Beam.' Her two companions introduced themselves as Betty Cridland and Barbara Harper.

'We'll give you some time to freshen up,' continued Mary. 'The coffee pot is steaming—you can have tea if you'd rather, Beth—and you can sample Betty's famous American-style hot biscuits.'

I drew the sheet over me that night, thinking I was much too tired to absorb new impressions, but as I lay on my side, gazing sleepily through the mosquito net and the mosquito-wire window, I was startled by the bright glory of the night sky. The radiant pageant of the constellations wheeled through the blackness of the night with a brilliance I had never before seen.

'It is true, Lord,' I murmured, as I turned over in bed. 'The heavens do declare Your glory; I give You praise and thanks. Bless my time at

Chali. Give me wisdom and understanding so that I may glorify You and bring Your blessing to these people.'

Not having had the opportunity to study tropical medicine as part of my preparation for mission, I had hoped to learn what I needed to know from the nurse who was permanently stationed there. Unfortunately, she had already left for a year's furlough in America. The thought of dealing with so many unknown factors, new diseases, unknown medications, languages—the list went on—muddled my mind. It was with trepidation that I accompanied Mary to the clinic early the next morning. A sizeable crowd of people were sitting on the ground, waiting to receive medical attention.

As if reading my thoughts, Mary stopped walking, turned to me and said, 'I know this must be a huge step for you, Beth. But you do have two great assets. First, you have the presence of God with you. Second, you have Kithgo—a young Uduk man who has been trained as a clinic assistant. He also speaks quite good English.'

'I can't tell you how relieved I am to hear that,' I said.

'Speaking of Kithgo, here he is.' Mary gestured towards a short, very dark-skinned Uduk who stepped forward with a friendly smile. What a gem he turned out to be—knowledgeable, capable and compassionate. We would become firm friends.

I WOULD SPEND most of my days working in the clinic with any who came for help. But there was much to learn. For example, I soon stopped testing urine for diabetes; Uduks did not have diabetes.

I was keen to find out all I could about the Uduk people, many of whom had turned from cruel ways and become Christians. Musa, the head of the church, gave me some of the background story. I was struck by the sincerity of his concluding statement.

'Before the mission came, we were sad. All but one of my children died when they were very young. Now our homes are warm with children.'

The Uduk people were comparatively short. Their language was soft and beautiful. I couldn't tell whether they were talking or singing. Their social structure was matrilineal—for example, when a woman gave birth, the biological father was not considered to be the child's relative or to have any control over the child's future. That role was reserved for the mother's brother.

When a man and a woman wished to couple, they would 'run off to the grass' and then live with each other as long as it suited them. There was no formal marriage ritual. The important person for a child was the mother's brother. Uduk women were vulnerable to theft, by men from other tribes whose dowry system made brides from their own tribes expensive and even unattainable.

The Uduks believed that twins, and the mother who bore them, were possessed by evil spirits, and that just one look from them could kill or curse. Until the government banned the practice, it had been their custom to bury mother and twins alive.

Once they became Christians, the people lost their fear. One of the Christian men actually prayed for his wife to have twins, in order to prove there was no need to fear.

His prayer was answered, but Susge, his wife, bore the brunt of the local reaction. The woman always bore the blame, and when Susge was blamed by the mother of a young boy who choked on a nut, the villagers were prevented from harming her, but it was a difficult life.

ONE NIGHT, my housemate, Grace, and I were asleep in the mosquito-wired sleep-out—it was often far too hot to sleep in our bedrooms in the house. Unless there was a prowling hyena, lion or leopard around, this was the favourite alternative.

I was suddenly awakened by a malevolent humming and the sensation that my body was being punctured by a hundred red hot needles. The sounds of feverish activity and anguished yelping from the other side of the sleep-out testified to the fact that Grace was also under attack.

In the torch light we soon discovered that driver ants by the million had invaded the house. The semi-demolished bodies of multitudes of former inhabitants of our hospitable sleep-out's thatched roof lay around us: a snake and a selection of scorpions. Clutching our sheets around us, Grace and I fled up the track, seeking refuge.

People say romantic things about thatched roofs—but from my experiences while living in Chali, I know they are nesting places for snakes, scorpions and bats.

I happen to regard bats as especially unusual and creepy things. At dusk, there would be a large dark cloud of them leaving the thatched roof of the house. The sky would be blackened as they escaped from the eaves. Occasionally, bats would get trapped in the room and fly around trying to find a way out. We had corrugated iron ceilings and I think it interfered with their radar. Sometimes, one landed on our beds at night. One of the most frightening things that I could imagine happening to me would be to have a bat fall on my face while I was asleep in bed.

We needed to be continually watchful where

we walked, and vigilant when we donned our shoes and clothing in the morning; scorpions loved hiding in shoes and clothes. They were an ever-present hazard. Though they were not exceptionally large, their sting was violently painful. Strong men cried for days after a sting.

Part of the house I shared was used as a children's nursery where we looked after twins who had been abandoned.

Beth (R) with a fellow missionary at Chali el Fil, holding two sets of twins who had been abandoned by their parents for fear of evil spirits. When missionaries were banished from the country, the Christian Uduks adopted them.

The nursery was also home to delightful, giggly, seven-month-old Lucy, who we were caring for because her mother had no breast milk. Her mother visited regularly, but could not care for Lucy at home because there were no local cows as the people were hunter-gatherers. When Lucy was old enough not to be dependent on milk, she would be given back to her mother.

Beth holding Lucy, a baby who was being temporarily raised by the mission because her mother had no breast milk.

I woke with a start one morning for no apparent reason. Without thinking, I rushed into the nursery where Lucy was sleeping. On her pillow, about three inches from her face—with its tail upraised to strike—was a scorpion. I grabbed her and rushed from the room, thanking God. A minute or so later and Lucy would have died in agony.

I was alone in the mission house one night when I was challenged by my first poisonous snake. I was fearful, but I found some heavy items to fling at it from a distance. It slithered away and disappeared from my sight. I wasn't sure where it went—and that was even more frightening! A few days later an appalling stench led me to a low and heavy cupboard—and its decaying body.

Beth's pile of luggage and supplies arriving at Chali el Fil

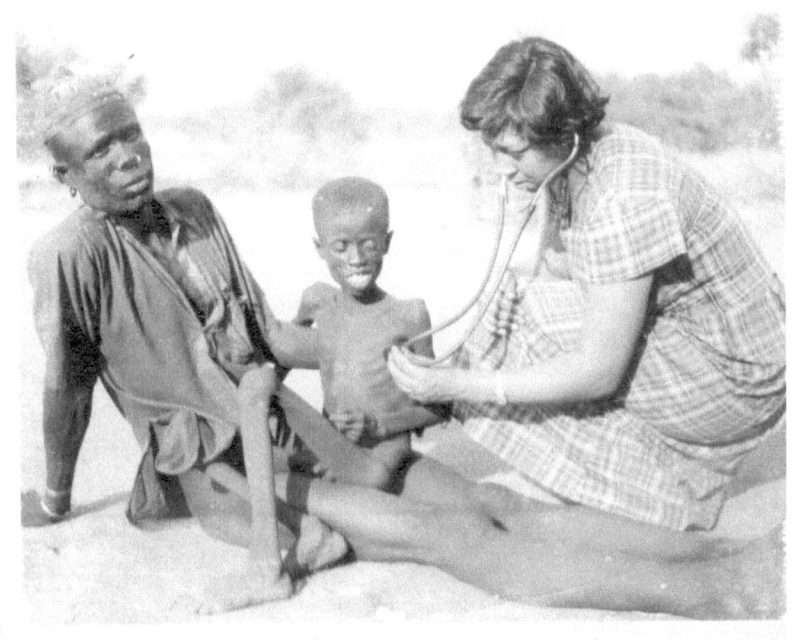

Beth assists a child and his father

The medical clinic at Chali el Fil

Beth with Kithgo—her amazing Uduk clinic helper

How the local mothers carried their babies

A village child playing with a ball

7

RESCUE BY DONKEY AND SHANK'S PONY

'Hello, Beth. It's Sam. I'm afraid we have some bad news. Mary-Helen's lost a little blood and we're afraid she will miscarry. We are very concerned. It's a lot to ask—especially with the roads closed—but could you possibly come to Yabus Bridge and help us?'

'Of course, Sam. I'll leave first thing in the morning. Is Mary-Helen in pain?'

'No, thank God. And the bleeding has stopped.'

'Excellent. Make sure she goes to bed and stays there. And please give her our love. We'll be praying for you.'

I put the handset down, and turned to face the three women who were looking anxiously at me. This crisis could not have happened at a more difficult time, and we prayed together for wisdom. Sam and Mary-Helen Burns, our nearest neighbours, were missionaries at Yabus Bridge: thirty miles of 'unoccupied' bushland away—unoccupied unless you counted lions, leopards, cobras, monkeys, and the crocodiles thriving in the Yabus River!

If Mary-Helen's emergency had occurred during the dry season, it would have meant no more than a bone-dislocating, two-and-a-half-hour drive in our once-green jeep over the pot-holed track, digging and sand-bagging our way through several dry watercourses.

However, this was not the dry season. It was the end of the rainy season.

The roads were closed. We were temporarily marooned on the mission station by the millions of transitory lakes, left behind by the torrents of water cascading down from the Ethiopian mountains throughout the rainy season. Our mission doctor and his family had returned to Canada because of his wife's allergy to the local ants; the small plane that usually rescued us in emergencies was under repair; I was the only midwife within several hundred square miles. The only solution was for me to go to Yabus Bridge as soon as possible—on donkey-back and shank's pony.

We assembled next morning in the pearlescent pre-dawn light. The misty-blue, jagged peaks of the Ethiopian mountains provided the dramatic backdrop for a scene dwarfed by a giant baobab tree, and a musical score that issued from the throats of awakening birds. At centrestage, a fidgety and sturdy grey male donkey carrying a monstrous, high-pommelled saddle on his back. To his left, three women with sober faces; to his right, five Uduk men with happy, toothy smiles, their beautiful, black skins oiled and shining, their spears sharpened to a lethal edge, and clustered around their feet, a miscellany of bags and cases containing food and drink, medical supplies and other necessities.

'Time to get on the donkey, Beth, and then we'll pray,' drawled the senior missionary, Mary Beam, her short, straight red hair lifting gently in the breeze.

As she spoke, the gravity of my situation suddenly struck home. I was setting out on a thirty-mile trek, to an unknown destination, through countryside resembling a cageless zoo, with five men I hardly knew, to face a crisis for which I would normally phone the doctor. To cap it all, at that moment my gaze collided with that of the donkey and I had the uncomfortable impression that he believed he had the situation under control. Although I had ridden horses in Australia, I had never negotiated a saddle with such a prominent pommel. And I had never encountered a donkey eye to eye! After an embarrassingly ungainly struggle, I was astride the saddle, holding tightly to the pommel.

As Mary began to pray, we closed our eyes reverently.

'Dear Lord, we ask you to—'

She stopped praying abruptly as strange sounds—snorts, cries and thumps—erupted from the direction of that most irreverent donkey and me. Mary and the others opened their eyes to see the saddle and me—in a tangled medley of arms, legs, and leather—on the ground beneath the triumphant donkey's belly.

I now understood the expression I had seen on his face when we looked at each other eye to eye. As Mary tightened the saddle-girth, he had inflated his stomach with air so that, at the appropriate moment, all he had to do was let the air go, stand with his weight on one side, then transfer it on the other, and enjoy the commotion that followed. Strangely, I developed a sense of respect for the wily beast during our short but event-filled relationship. I am sure that he felt no hostility towards me personally; it was merely a battle of wits—and he had definitively won the first round!

We'll see about that, I thought to myself… and I certainly did!

WITHIN HALF AN HOUR, we were on the track and passing through very pleasant countryside: green, lightly wooded and studded with impressive rock formations. I could have imagined myself back home in Australia—apart from the absence of eucalyptus trees.

Suddenly, off to our right, a small herd of Thomson's gazelle sprang to life, leaping in their inimitably graceful fashion. My heart sang. This really was Africa, and God had called me here to give help where it was needed. I knew that God would give me the wisdom I lacked in this and all the situations I faced.

I was eager to get to know my travelling companions. The Uduk people I had met seemed to be gentle and rather small—in contrast to my expectations. The men were about my height: five feet, six inches. In the tribal situation, I knew the men were naked and the women wore a small beaded cloth, looped over a string around their waist. There had been a Christian mission station at Chali for many years. Christian Uduks often wore clothing received from America in missionary barrels. The Uduk men travelling with me were dressed in a surprising array of clothes—we were indeed a colourful crew!

Two of the men accompanying me, Musa and Kithgo, were mature Christians who, fortunately for me, spoke quite good English.

'Is your heart happy at Chali?' I asked grey-haired Musa. A smile stretched his whole face.

'Yes, plenty happy.'

'I am very happy too, Musa,' I replied. I smiled, and, because I didn't know how to continue the conversation, I rode on in silence. Besides, my being mounted on a donkey made easy conversation with the men walking in front and behind me difficult.

I had aptly named the donkey Abe after Abraham in the Bible who also 'knew not where he was going' (from Hebrews 11:8). The donkey and I plodded on in silence, one frustratingly short step after the other, until we encountered some local 'roadworks': twenty or more Uduk men squatting on the track removing weeds with hand-hoes and, theoretically, filling the potholes with earth. Ahead of us stretched a mile or more of the dark brown 'road' they had already cleared. I had my suspicions about how effective their repair of the potholes was. My suspicions were confirmed within a few metres of the start of the 'road'!

I had heard that the correct technique for riding on this style of stirrup-less saddle was to perch precariously on it, crossing the ankles over the animal's neck. I tried to concentrate on the countryside around me.

You can imagine what happened when Abe

put his foot in a grass-filled pothole. Down Abe went—and over his head I flew!

No-one could ever complain that the Uduks lack a sense of humour. They exploded with laughter, literally holding their sides. Abe was unperturbed. Fortunately, there was no great damage to anything but my dignity, but I would sit gingerly for the next week or two.

The day grew hotter. The cleared area of the road was behind us. After my recent experience, I was now walking beside the triumphantly strutting Abe. We came to an area of damp earth that was overgrown with elephant grass. It was tall, at least two feet above my head. The sunlight flowed through the translucent green leaves as I moved through them. It was as though I was parting the waves of a delicately green, luminous sea, so entrancing that the euphoria remains with me after more than sixty years.

About midday, shimmering through the heat haze, there appeared before us a cluster of gnarled tree trunks. Their sparse, deep-green canopies promised blissful shade from the heat of the sun. The men spoke together and Kithgo reported their decision.

'It is good we stop here and eat, but very soon we must walk on. It is still very far. It is best to be at Yabus before sundown and many animals wake.'

We were all anxious for news of Mary-Helen

and the baby. It was comforting, therefore, when Musa followed the thanksgiving for lunch with heartfelt prayers for the family in crisis, and for a safe journey for us all. There were smiles all round as we reflected on the nearness of our Father God, and relished our oneness as members of God's family. My sandwiches and cake quickly despatched, and in line with Kithgo's wise advice, we were soon back on the track.

Once more in the saddle, the combined effects of Abe's steady gait and the normal afternoon post-lunch languor—not to mention the early start to my day—induced a dangerous drowsiness in me. I refused to allow myself to consider the unspeakable indignity of falling asleep and falling off Abe again. Besides, the score would then be three-nil, and Abe's smirk would be intolerable!

I knew I had to find the means of staying awake to maintain some dignity. *Mind power is the answer*, I told myself firmly. I forced myself to think back to the day, four months ago, when I stepped out of the chilly plane onto the melting tarmac of the Khartoum runway.

I thought back to our great excitement when we learned that Mary-Helen and Sam Burns were coming to the SIM administration centre in Khartoum for medical tests. Everyone loved the couple. Sam, a genial ex-army Irishman, and Mary-Helen, an American, had been in their early forties when they met and fell in love in the Sudan. Their romance and marriage had lifted the spirits of their missionary colleagues, and nothing could have been more satisfying than the news of Mary-Helen's pregnancy.

Of course, I'd had a thousand questions to ask when I initially met them in Khartoum and knew where they were stationed in relation to Chali el Fil, but I had been too shy. What is it like down south? Are the people friendly? What are the most frequent medical problems?

Perhaps they had seen the hopeful look on my face.

'Sam and I wonder if you have any questions you'd like to ask us?' Mary-Helen said. 'We're free this afternoon.'

We settled down in the comfortable chairs of the mission centre lounge, shortly after lunch. Mary-Helen put her feet up, and smiled at me expectantly.

'I've heard that you have some exciting animal stories,' I began, diffidently. 'Please tell me one of those—children from home are always asking me about lions.'

'That's easy,' answered Sam. 'Let's tell Beth about our walk from Yabus Bridge to Chali.'

'I was thinking the same. I'm sure you'll find it interesting, Beth.'

'This happened when we were courting,' Sam began. 'I worked at Chali and Mary-Helen was stationed at Yabus Bridge, thirty miles away. In the rainy season the roads are closed so the only way for us to see each other was for me to walk to Yabus Bridge. As usual, when it was time for me to return to Chali, Mary-Helen would always walk the first two or three miles with me.

'This day we left Yabus very early. There were about a dozen of us: Uduks from Chali and Hill-Baruns from Yabus Bridge who were our guides and protectors, Mary-Helen and myself, and Yusif, a twelve-year-old Hill-Barun lad, who was devoted to Mary-Helen and had begged to come along with us.'

Sam paused to breathe, and Mary-Helen explained about her relationship with the boy.

'Yusif had almost died of dysentery, two years before. I treated him at the medical centre, and he recovered. He appointed himself as my protector.'

Sam continued the story.

'It must have been a beautiful, clear morning—but Mary-Helen and I were oblivious to everything but each other. We were planning our wedding. As we rounded a bend in the track, our guides stopped short, held us back, and signalled urgently for silence.

'As we looked where they were pointing. I think my heart stopped beating.

'There, resting among the bushes not far from the road, was a pride of five lions. I could see the massive head of the male as he lay, relaxed and apparently asleep, surrounded by his pride.

'Every instinct within us told us to stop, turn around quietly, and sneak back the way we had come.

'Everyone stopped. That is, everyone but Yusif!

'He had been walking some yards ahead of the rest of us. We couldn't believe it when we saw him glance casually toward the lions and continue calmly on his way. We realised that we had no choice but to follow him. I gripped Mary-Helen's hand as we began what seemed to be the longest, most chilling walk of our lives.

'The lions didn't stir.

'When we caught up with Yusif, we asked him, "Why did you walk past the lions? Weren't you scared?" "No, I wasn't," he answered, sunnily. "Why ever not?" "Because I knew you were behind."

'I never found out what he meant by that comment,' said Sam pensively. 'Was he remembering the biblical story of Daniel in the lion's den? Or did he think that no self-respecting lion would settle for a skinny kid when he could choose a plump missionary instead?'

'We knew it was a miracle,' protested Mary-Helen. 'God shut the mouths of the lions for Daniel—and God must have done more for us.

God shut their ears and noses, too—they never stirred, not one of them. I was watching.'

Although I heard the story in the safety of the mission house in Khartoum, I still shivered with fear. It was much more realistic now that I was on the actual road to Yabus Bridge, very close to where the incident had occurred. How do the local people deal with the possibility of meeting a lion, I wondered. I called to Kithgo to ask him.

'Which is the most frightening animal you can meet, Kithgo? A lion?'

'No. Better meet a lion than a leopard.'

'Why is that?'

'The lion, he thinks too much.'

'I don't understand. What do you mean?'

'Sometimes you can trick a lion. If I meet a lion, I call out like this.' Kithgo cupped his hands around his mouth uttering a piercing, high-pitched cry. 'Twee-lee-lee-lee-lee-lee-lee-lee, Musa! Susge! Come here.'

'Then what happens?' I asked.

'Perhaps the lion, he say to himself: Kithgo not by himself; he has friends here to help. So the lion he goes away. But if I meet a leopard, he not think like the lion. He always angry. Nothing I can do. I just sit and wait.'

'Thank you, Kithgo,' I said. 'I don't want to meet a lion or a leopard, today. What about you?'

'I am the same as you.'

I was distracted by my thoughts, and, before I noticed it, Abe had begun the descent into the creek. There was no time to dismount.

Déjà vu! Surely it couldn't happen again—for a third time?

Alas it could. And it did—it's the absolute truth.

This time I really appreciated Abe's tolerance. With quiet and passive resignation, he allowed me to slip sedately over his tail without lifting a hoof. I walked for the next few miles to reward him.

Thankfully, the sun was dropping in the west. The torrid heat of the day was abating. A variety of birds were making their late afternoon calls and the scenery was changing as we approached the Yabus River. The bushy plain was replaced by huge trees from which the strident voices of the colobus monkeys rent the air as they squabbled with each other and shrieked their disapproval of our presence. What a dramatic sight they presented, their black faces framed by wide, white ruffs. Around their black, furry backs hung white 'shawls'—perhaps fifteen to twenty centimetres long. Their substantial tufted tails were longer than their bodies. Once you've seen a colobus monkey, you'll never forget it.

Despite being known widely as Yabus Bridge, the 'bridge' part of the name is a euphemism for a deep ford. When we arrived at the ford, it was covered by more than a metre of freely flowing water. After our guides had scouted the water for crocodiles, we waded through safely to the other side.

Thankfully, Sam was waiting on the opposite bank, anxious to greet his wet, dirty, dishevelled and weary guests with a happy smile—and heart-warming news.

'Mary-Helen's fine! She's resting comfortably and there's no further problems. Thank the Lord.'

I WAS VERY impressed with their house, especially the mosquito trap: a sort of double door that allowed humans to enter—and kept mosquitoes out! The beautiful, big picture windows looked out over the Yabus River. Mosquito netting once again: glass wouldn't have survived the trip.

When I commented on the glass-free windows, Sam and Mary-Helen told me the story about the sick dog they housed in the passage outside their bedroom. They were woken by low growling, followed by a crash and a yelp. When they went to check what had happened, their dog was gone. The bloody paw prints suggested that a leopard leapt through the mosquito netting, picked up the dog, and left the same way. Fortunately, the sick baby in another room nearby had escaped the same fate. And so had Sam and Mary-Helen.

The night after their dog disappeared, they were both woken by a soft, rather apologetic, coughing sound. When Sam cautiously looked out through the bedroom window, he saw a leopard in the moonlight—sitting only a few feet from their mosquito-netting windows. Sam and Mary-Helen surmised that the big cat had probably come back for another dog!

The only way the bedroom windows could be secured against a determined predator was to attach heavy wooden shutters to the outside of the window frames—from outside the house.

Though they had repaired the mosquito netting in the passage window, and had the sick baby sleeping in a cot in their room, they had a very scary night. They decided the best strategy was to stay in their bedroom, keep watch—and wait quietly for the leopard to leave.

Sam decided he'd have to do something in case the leopard returned the following night. He found a gun and kept it next to the bed. Fortunately, the leopard didn't return.

AFTER BREAKFAST, following a restless night—I could not forget the frailty of mosquito-netting windows—I sat down at Mary-Helen's bedside. Conscientiously trying to ignore the three crocodiles sunning themselves on the bank where we had crossed the river the previous evening, I questioned her about her medical history.

'Have you ever had abdominal problems, Mary-Helen?'

Looking a little embarrassed, she replied, 'Yes, I'm afraid I have—ever since I was ten years old.'

'What happened?'

'The circus was in town, and we already had our tickets. My brother and I were counting the hours until the show began. There was no way I was going to risk missing out by telling my mother about my bad stomach-ache. Sadly, I was so ill that I didn't enjoy the show. I almost died from peritonitis—my appendix ruptured. I smelt so bad that they had to nurse me on the balcony! I've had trouble with my stomach ever since.'

'What a price to pay for a visit to the circus! I believe you have problems that could endanger you and the baby. You must rest now—and return to America as soon as possible.'

'Yes, I know,' she whispered, wiping her tears away. 'I am so disappointed. This is my home now.'

A few days later, Mary-Helen told me the good news.

'There was a message this morning to say that

the plane is fixed and will pick Sam and me up in a couple of days to take us to Khartoum. We'll fly to the States from there.'

'Thank God. I am so pleased this has worked out so well for you. Your mother will be so happy.'

'Yes, she will. But there's more good news—for you. The plane will come back here to pick you up and fly you back to Chali.' Mary-Helen's rather damp smile turned to laughter at my expression.

Two days later, I waved goodbye to my friends Mary-Helen and Sam as the small Cessna carried them back to Khartoum.

There was another who had good reason to be as pleased as I was that I would be flying back to Chali—and that was Abe. I whispered the good tidings into his twitching ear as he chomped on the carrot I had smuggled to him.

I was *almost* sure he smiled.

8

FROM CHALI EL FIL TO ABAIYAT

My twelve months at Chali with the Uduk people came to an end and I was appointed to work several hundred miles away with a different tribe of people, the Dinkas, near the small village of Abaiyat.

After some sad farewells to the local Uduk people and the fellow missionaries with whom I had been working, a small plane whisked me away for a month's holiday to lovely Lake Bishoftu in cool Ethiopia.

Refreshed and eager to begin work, I noticed that the countryside over which we were flying was totally different from that near Chali. Gone were the trees; beneath our wings was an immense grassy plain.

The only signs of habitation in my new home were our mission station with its three houses and girdle of trees planted by missionaries and, a kilometre distant, the small village of Abaiyat with its mud-and-grass huts.

I was told that trees were feared because of the spirits that occupied them. Apart from the single stunted tree in the village with its girdle of placating fetishes there were no other trees in sight, just grass. And not a surfaced road or a river within many miles.

During the rainy season, water from the White Nile flooded the Dinka plains. The mission station was cut off for maybe three or four months every year because all the roads were closed. Surrounded by small water courses, we waded through the mud and marvelled at the occasional fish. I believe this potentially sodden area stretches for about 300 miles across Africa.

Our mission station comprised two brick, two-bedroom cottages with mosquito net windows and sleep-outs—which Carol and I viewed with suspicion—a small brick clinic, and some sheds lining the dirt track.

About a hundred-and-fifty metres from our station buildings, Bill, the senior missionary, had recently supervised the building of six mud huts. They were intended for the sick people who were carried—often for long distances—into the station for treatment.

In this part of Africa, finding medical help was very difficult. When people heard by word of mouth that there was medicine at Abaiyat, they travelled long distances to get to our station from their villages dotted throughout the vast Dinka plains. There was really no other medical help within hundreds of square miles—maybe more. They would make a bed of the stems of reeds they carried on their heads.

Some officials came to our clinic and asked for 'some of the medicine you keep for yourselves, not what you give to them'. They were incredulous when told that the medicine we used for ourselves was exactly the same as the medicine we provided for the local people. (I believe such attitudes to the tribal people in the south have disappeared since the northern and southern regions became separate independent nations.)

The beliefs of the Dinka people did not match western ideas, especially about disease.

On washing days, the Dinkas wouldn't walk on the track that went between our house and the clinic, because the smell of the soap was so awful to them.

A Dinka man told me that his people had a different concept about sickness. To them it was the result of evil spirits or a curse that had been placed. When we walked along a path, we saw many grass knots which had apparently been dropped in the pathway of an enemy to bring sickness or ill fortune.

Their attitude to medicine was pragmatic: 'Well, we've tried the witch doctor. That didn't work, his spirit wasn't strong enough. So we'll go to the mission and try the spirit of Jesus Christ.'

If our medicine didn't work, they would say, 'Oh, you couldn't help it: the spirit was not strong enough.' And this also meant that although they would come and get medicine from us, they might not take it, because their disloyalty might anger the local spirits.

Come with me on a typical journey: an early morning visit to the clinic to ensure a teenage girl, very ill with pneumonia, received her penicillin shot.

When the alarm woke me at two in the morning, I sat up in bed and reached under my pillow for the torch, searching the room carefully —ceiling, bed, and floor—for scorpions, snakes and other wildlife. After giving my slippers a good shake, followed by a careful visual inspection by torchlight, I was convinced at last that there were no lurking scorpions—there were no shining eyes. I donned my slippers and went to face my next challenge: waking my fellow missionary, Geraldine. In Abaiyat, I never walked anywhere without slippers, shoes or boots.

Gerry was a trifle deaf, and it took a gentle touch before she opened her eyes.

'Hi, Gerry. It's two o'clock.'

'Already? I've hardly closed my eyes. I was

having a great dream too, all about California. But I'm awake now.'

'The first thing to do is light the Coleman lamp. I've never done it before, sorry. Could you do it for me, please?'

'That's okay. Glad to help. They're not as dangerous as they sound—and I'd sure feel happier with a Coleman than a torch.'

While Gerry went off to find the lamp and the matches, I thought about the job ahead. I appreciated Gerry's insistence that we light the lamp despite the time it took in the middle of the night. Only a month ago, lions and hyenas had been fighting noisily between the mission houses. The victorious lions left behind a hyena with a broken leg, vomiting against our living room wall. Bill had to dispose of it in the morning.

Shhh-shhh-shhh: the Coleman lamp hissed into life. It was time for our adventure. This was the first of many ventures into the darkness, with a lamp and our medical supplies. Fortunately, we never met any big cats during our night-time missions.

At Chali, Kithgo—the Uduk clinic assistant—had known the people. He spoke English very well as he'd been taught by a missionary. He was absolutely indispensable to me for the twelve months I worked in the Chali clinic.

In Abaiyat, my clinic assistant, Aweer, also spoke English well and was equally indispensable.

Andrew Aweer—Beth's Dinka clinic helper at Abaiyat

The Dinka language was complex for non-native speakers. It was a spoken language and hadn't been written down, except for a translation of the Scriptures into Dinka. As well as having ten ways of making plurals from singulars, the language had different degrees of breathiness, and words spoken in a higher or lower register had different meanings.

One Dinka was astonished when he asked one of our missionaries a question about American marriage customs. 'We pay for our women with cows. What do you pay for your wives?'

Travis, young and romantic, was sure he'd answered, 'We pay with our love.'

Every Dinka exploded with laughter, until one of them stopped laughing long enough to ask, 'How many?'

Travis discovered to his blushing embarrassment that the Dinka words for 'love' and 'turtles' are almost indistinguishable to foreigners.

Even experienced Dinka speakers could make mistakes. I couldn't be quite sure what I was saying, so I was careful when using Dinka—I sought Aweer's help whenever I could.

It intrigued me to discover that Aweer had formerly been an assistant to a local witch doctor. He told me that the Dinka 'doctor' he had worked for would kill a chicken, take a sinew out of it and hide it in his cheek. He'd suck the patient's wound and pull the chicken sinew out of his mouth claiming a cure because he'd extracted this 'worm' from his client, and demand a fat fee.

When Aweer began working for the missionaries, he waited expectantly and in vain to learn our tricks. He became a faithful believer in Christ.

It was very interesting talking to Aweer about his people. The Dinka people's beliefs in evil spirits governed many aspects of their lives. The ability of individuals to put curses on others made them afraid of each other. Of course, we read in the Christian Scriptures that many things are caused by spirits—and we in the West don't give enough credence to the diverse spiritual influences on our lives.

DURING ONLY ONE of my six years among the Dinka was there a doctor on call. Unfortunately, his wife was very allergic to the local ants—and there are many ants on the Dinka plains. After her allergic reaction to an ant bite, her husband recognised that being bitten even once more could result in her death from anaphylactic shock. Because of this they had to go back to Canada after only a year, though he and his family loved the Sudan. Another doctor was never sent to replace him while I was at Abaiyat.

I was there without access to medical support. I estimate there was no Western doctor within many thousand square miles. Fortunately, a lot of the diseases I encountered were very obvious: chest infections; various animal bites including leopard bites; crocodile bites. However, we did have specific medicine to treat leprosy, a common skin disease in the area.

Despite the range of experience and training among the nurses I worked with, none of us had the medical training and capacity to diagnose some of the local diseases—many of which neither the American nurses, nor I, had come across in our training. We were grateful for the miracles brought by antibiotics that were suitable for a wide range of problems.

With so many sicknesses and no doctor close by to consult about the symptoms we were trying to manage, we were working blind a lot of the time. I believe no real work had been done on the diseases prevalent in the area before this time.

Perhaps the most prevalent and dangerous disease was amoebic dysentery. People affected by the single-celled parasite *Entamoeba histolytica* could go downhill very rapidly. I speak from personal experience.

Not long after I reached the Sudan, while still in Khartoum, I succumbed—probably from the food I was eating or the water I was drinking. It can also be caught from contact with others affected by the parasite.

The first thing I knew, the floor came up and hit me. I had no sense of having fallen. My temperature was way too high—104^0F ($40°C$)—and I was very sick for a few days. The mission staff told me they were about to notify my parents of the seriousness of my illness when I began to show improvement.

My treatments did not always agree with Dinka practice.

When Deng came in with a spear wound to his forehead, I stitched it up and gave him antibiotics, and then explained that the wound would heal really well.

A concentration crease appeared on Deng's wounded scalp and he went out hurriedly.

Aweer informed me that he had gone to remove the stitches. 'You don't understand, Aduei (my Dinka name, pronounced Adway),' stated Aweer, pityingly. 'Dinkas love their scars from a fight. When your son is older, he will come to you and ask, "Father, where are your scars from fighting?" If you have no scars you must just sit, in shame.'

The costly bride price—thirty cows for a prize bride—was hard for a Dinka to find, especially if there were no girls in his family to bring a dowry. If an older son died without producing a son to carry on his name, his younger brother must be married and produce children in the older brother's stead. This would require him to find thirty cows for his dead brother's dowry and have children in his brother's name, before he could find thirty cows for himself. That is a total of sixty cows for his own wife and to have children in his own name. Many faced the sadness that their own name would 'go into the ground'.

I wondered what use my midwifery course

would be. The answer was, very little, apart from Mary Helen's problem. There was just the one case at Abaiyat.

I was leaving the clinic one hot summer's day when a woman appeared. As she approached, I could see she had difficulty walking and had wrapped a cloth around her legs.

I reopened the clinic door and we went inside. The exhausted woman pulled the cloth aside.

I was shocked to see, protruding from her body, the arm and shoulder of a dead baby. I was also afraid. There was no doctor, no hospital and, theoretically, no way the baby could be born. The measurement of head and chest was too great.

My prayers have never been more fervent as I knelt down, grasped the baby's torso and pulled.

The baby was delivered. The mother's uterus did not come with it. There was no bleeding—just a jubilant woman who had been released from a terrible situation, a few incredulous onlookers, and a praising, thankful midwife.

Dinka ambulance at Abaiyat, having carried their friend many miles to seek help from the mission clinic

Rev Gideon Adwok—the Christian pastor of the local church who was martyred after the missionaries were expelled

Beth greets a Dinka friend at Abaiyat

American missionaries Geraldine and Bill with Beth (back R) and a group of Dinkas playing sport

Missionary Geraldine showing her camera to the local Dinkas

Dinka plain in the rainy season

Rainy season with a grass hut and a woman carrying water

Abaiyat village

Beth at Abaiyat surrounded by local Dinka children

A group of Christians from the Blue Nile area

A missionary plane bringing supplies in the dry season

Dinka people in ceremonial dress

9

LEAVING HOME, COMING HOME

During my sixth year in the Sudan, like most of the people in our mission I succumbed to hepatitis. I was sent back to Australia to have tests, because little scientific medical work had been done in relation to the diseases of the Sudan. It was hoped that my test results would be helpful.

As the plane rose I marvelled, for the last time, at the surrender of the identities of the Blue and White Niles, lost in the clashing birth pangs of the longest river on earth.

'Surely my work in Africa was not meant to end this way,' I thought sadly; I had expected to spend my life in the Sudan. As Khartoum disappeared, I was certain I would never see the city or the people I loved again, and I was right. Shortly after I was sent home in 1961, SIM missionaries were expelled from southern Sudan.

In the late 1950s, Anglo-Egyptian Sudan had gained its independence. Egypt had governed the northern half, now known as the Republic of Sudan: an Islamic state populated with Arabs. The northern half was united by one language. Though there were different shades of Islam within the republic and they didn't always get on well with each other, their common language meant they could communicate relatively easily.

In contrast, the southern half, governed by England, consisted of hundreds of tribes, speaking different languages, with different customs, beliefs and religious traditions. When the Sudan gained its independence, the southerners rioted, wanting the English to stay. Many people —including Christians—were martyred in the first Sudanese civil war. After a second civil war, in 2011 the Republic of South Sudan gained independence from the Islamic northern republic.

The forced exit of Christian missionaries in 1961 was not unexpected. The government threatened to expel mission staff periodically. Several times, we were packed up and ready to go before we received a reprieve. The last few months I was in the Sudan had been like living in a seething pot ready to boil over.

When I arrived back in Australia, I didn't fit into the culture anymore. I missed the familiarity of life in the sparsely populated plains of Sudan.

If you pointed to anything with your finger amongst the tribespeople, you were putting a curse on them, so you never pointed with your finger. You stuck out your tongue and pointed with the tip in the direction of the item you wanted. I remember the look of surprise on the shopkeeper's face the first time I went into a shop in Adelaide and said, 'I want that scarf,' and stuck out my tongue. You get so used to doing this in Sudan. Dinkas also wouldn't step over anyone's feet because that would put a curse on them. So I'd be in the picture theatre and I'd wait for people to pull their feet way back so I could get to a vacant seat. When they didn't respond to the visual cue, I'd say, 'Excuse me'—and they'd look at me as if I was weird, a foreigner.

My mother needed me—she was eighty-five and alone. My parents had been separated for many years. Though they had tried to get back together while I was in the Sudan, their attempted reunion didn't work. I have a picture my mother sent me of them together during this attempt to rebuild their relationship.

Beth's parents, Bert and Lily Wordie, during their reconciliation

They were happy for a short time, and I realised for the first time the warm feeling of belonging this brought, compared to the insecurity and lack of connection I experienced throughout my childhood. However, their old differences sprang up again and they soon separated for good.

After a month or so of having been prodded, pricked and biopsied in Melbourne, and the tests having been analysed, the doctor's verdict was that I could not return to nursing for some months. It took me a long time to recover from hepatitis—and I never did go back to nursing. I was yellow and lethargic. My liver was twice its normal size. I slept with a huge dictionary under my right side for support—and was not impressed when asked to do the ironing for the Melbourne mission home. I was fragile and sick and the 1960s iron was very heavy.

Beth's mother, Lily Wordie, after Beth's return from Sudan.

When I returned to Adelaide, I found a little flat only a short way from my mother's house so that I could be near her.

I didn't know what to do next. I talked about my situation with a friend of mine, Joan, whom I had known from high school days and who had supported me faithfully during my years in Africa.

Joan invited me to her home, and after we had eaten and caught up on the past she asked, 'What are you going to do now, Beth?'

'That's a problem. I can't go back to nursing for months and I can't expect the mission society to support me. I'm sure God has a plan.'

'There's no doubt about that. By the way, I've got some news, too. I've resigned from my job after nearly twenty years,' said Joan, smiling at my amazement.

'Really, do you mean it? Why?'

'I want to do something different with my life and I'm going to start a course in social work.'

'I've never heard of social work,' I said. 'What is it?'

As Joan began to explain the course she had enrolled in, I became more and more interested. I had been thinking that study would be one thing I could do as I convalesced, but I didn't know of any avenue of study that would be suitable for me. I hadn't heard about social work before, yet when Joan told me I had to sign up by the end of the next day to study this year, I left her place and drove straight to the Adelaide inner city.

Driving down North Terrace, I prayed for a car park near the University of Adelaide because I couldn't walk far. When I found one within range, I rushed to the enrolment centre and signed up for a Diploma of Social Work. I had very little money to pay for the course, but I was offered a scholarship—without it, I wouldn't have been able to take up a place in the course.

I was still sick. I still had hepatitis and I felt far from being able to study. I hadn't studied for many years, so I used all the exam gimmicks and mnemonics to get through the tests and exams. As I completed the assessments for first year of study, I felt I had failed. In the early 1960s, if you didn't think you had passed you could apply for supplementary exams—I applied for supplementaries in all my subjects even before the results came out.

Imagine my surprise and delight when I found that I had topped biology and come second or third in economics. I received high credits for psychology and history. God blessed me so much in my studies.

AFTER COMPLETING my social work diploma, I obtained a position at the Queen Elizabeth Hospital (QEH) as a senior social worker. Despite my success as a student, I was still lacking in confidence.

One day the wife of the CEO of the hospital approached me. I believe she had been an army nurse—she always called me by my surname, even when we met socially. She spoke in a voice that suggested she would accept no compromise. 'Wordie, you must join the Penguin Club.'

I don't think it ever occurred to her that anyone would say no to her 'invitations', which were motivated by kindness.

'Yes,' I murmured dutifully. 'What is the Penguin Club?'

'It is the club where they train women public speakers. There is a meeting next Tuesday in Adelaide. I'm going, and I'll take you with me.'

True to her word, she picked me up the following Tuesday at lunchtime and escorted me to the meeting room. A group of well-dressed women of varying ages, wearing hats and gloves, sat around a table on which reposed books, papers and a shiny brass bell.

We took our seats and the chairperson rang the bell. After the formalities, the real business of the meeting began, namely the presentation of speeches by members who had been allotted their topic at the previous meeting. The Penguin Club was designed to teach women formal meeting procedures and to accustom them to speaking in public.

This marked the beginning of a fifty-year association with the Penguin Club. I was State President for a term, and was challenged to speak about a diverse range of topics, from 'a dose of salts' to 'the Roman army marched on their stomach'.

I BEGAN my work at QEH, where the doctors referred a forty-one-year-old German woman, Annelore, to me for assistance. I was immediately drawn to this lady whose pain-filled brown eyes revealed the depth of her suffering. She had just been diagnosed with leukaemia.

Annelore had migrated to Australia with her English husband several years before. They had four children aged between eight and eighteen years. She had not seen her parents for a number of years, and desperately longed to visit them in Germany while she was still well enough to travel. Knowing that her husband and family would need all their resources in the event of her death, she came to me to explore the possibility of raising the money by public subscription.

An appeal was launched, and it was successful. Annelore visited her parents in Germany. On her return, she visited me each time she came for her hospital check-ups.

Her strength and optimism were inspiring. She put her flagging energy into making clothes for the children and preparing Christmas puddings and other special treats for them. Her doctors were also impressed by her positive outlook, and introduced her to other leukaemia patients who appreciated the encouragement of this caring, gently-spoken lady.

She told me of the family interest in stamp collecting and I would save any interesting stamps for them.

As Annelore showed me pictures of the four children, I sensed her love for them, her desire to protect them from grief—and her sorrow that she would not participate in their future.

I WAS STILL a junior member of the Penguin Club when I came across an invitation from the English Speaking Union to apply for a scholarship to visit the New Zealand branch. The trip included travelling to several cities, giving speeches at their meetings. My application was accepted, and I left on a flight to New Zealand with a mixture of fear and excitement.

The trip included an invitation to the Waitangi Celebration in the magnificent Bay of Islands, which commemorated the treaty between the Maori and the British colonists.

It was an excellent experience. I was received with kindness and stayed in beautiful homes of people who were typically wealthy and enjoyed a higher social status than was usual for me.

Beth at the time of her scholarship trip to New Zealand, and a newspaper clipping. Text: 'English Speaking Union scholarship winner, Miss Elizabeth Wordie, who leaves on Tuesday for a month's study tour of New Zealand, was guest of honour at a luncheon yesterday in the ESU clubrooms, North Terrace. Miss Wordie is senior social worker at The Queen Elizabeth Hospital.'

I remember one visit with mixed feelings. It was the opening of the oyster season and I was invited to a lavish luncheon. The purity of the starched tablecloths, the gleam of the crystal glasses, the mirror brilliance and quantity of silverware on the table was unfamiliar. I was doing my best to live up to the high social status of the august event, but my pride was to suffer a humiliating fall.

I was escorted by an elegant and gracious silken-clad lady, and we drove in her equally immaculate Bentley to the restaurant, where I was urged to sample the oysters.

We'd no sooner set out on our way home when I suddenly felt extremely ill. Urgently, I called for the driver to stop the limousine. I opened the immaculate door, sat in the gutter, and vomited! The elegant and gracious lady and her expressionless chauffeur both coped magnificently!

My departure from New Zealand was another debacle. The airport was crowded. I waited in the long queue for some time. When I finally presented my ticket to the official, he took one look at me, examined my ticket closely, looked at me with a frown, and said, in a low voice, 'I must ask you to wait here for a moment, while I talk to my senior officer.'

The official from the English Speaking Union who had accompanied me started to look rather uncomfortable as I stepped to the side. A few minutes later, another airport official conducted me to a side room.

'No doubt you've heard of the White Australia policy. I'll have to check with Australian officials before you'll be permitted to board the plane to fly to Australia at this time. Some people have been sent back.'

The ESU official was obviously upset and angry and tried to remonstrate on my behalf. The New Zealand official remained firm.

'I'm sorry, Madame,' he said, 'but this is part of our procedural arrangements with Australian officials that I cannot change. We have had some people returned to us in the past.'

I sat wondering what would happen next. I was reassured and relieved by the answer that came some time later.

'We have checked with Australian immigration officials. You are a bona fide Australian citizen. You may proceed to the departure lounge, and board the plane. Thank you for your patience. We apologise for any inconvenience.'

Finally, I had boarded the plane and was on my way home—with a new understanding of what it must feel like to be stateless.

I returned to work with a selection of picturesque stamps collected in New Zealand, anticipating the way Annelore's eyes would light up with interest when she saw them. How sad I was to learn that Annelore had died, and that the QEH had ceased contact with the family. I never forgot her, and prayed for the wellbeing of her husband and children. I thought about contacting them, but it had been several weeks. I decided not to.

10

A PARTNER IN THE DANCE

*I*t was in 1969 that I decided to go to a ballroom dancing class with my friend Susan, a scientist from the University of Adelaide.

The music was good, the atmosphere light-hearted, and the dance instructor patient with our rather clumsy efforts to discipline our feet. Susan and I, both a little breathless, sat sipping cold lemonade and watching the brightly clad couples swirl and sway. I noticed a tall, attractive man with light brown, curly hair guiding his partner with smooth expertise through the whirling throng. I was admiring his prowess and thinking he was probably about my age, when Susan grabbed my arm.

'See that man—the good dancer? He works

at the university. I know him quite well. When the dance finishes, I'll call him over.'

After he had returned his partner to her seat, true to her word the uninhibited Susan stood up, waved and beckoned. The man hesitated, then came towards us, smiling.

'Hello Susan. Sorry, I didn't recognise you at first.'

'You're quite a dancer! I'm pleased to see you enjoying yourself. This is my friend, Beth Wordie. Beth, this is Albert Robertson.'

'Hello, Beth,' said Albert. He had a pleasant English accent.

My mouth opened, I fought for breath, and finally stammered, breathlessly, 'H-h-hello, Albert. It's good to meet you.'

If Susan and Albert noticed my confusion, they were too polite to comment. It wasn't the time or place to reveal that I had been the social worker to his late wife, Annelore, and had even spoken to him on the phone.

Albert then invited each of us to dance with him. When my turn came, my already favourable impression of him was strongly reinforced. He was easy to talk to, courteous and considerate. And handsome. I wanted, so much, to get to know him better.

My opportunity came with the close of the dance session. Susan left immediately for a prior engagement. When Albert made the suggestion that we go for a coffee, I was quick to agree. We settled down at a table and after some light conversation, it was time to explain myself.

'I wondered whether you noticed my reaction when I heard your name?'

'Well yes, I did—and I was puzzled. We haven't met before, have we?'

'No, but I have actually spoken to you on the phone. I feel that I almost know you and your family.'

'Now I'm really curious,' said Albert.

'I am a social worker at the Queen Elizabeth Hospital, and I used to see Annelore when she came for her medical check-ups. I was very sad to learn of her death and I often thought about you and your family. She was an amazing woman who inspired us all with her courage.' Annelore had died two years before.

'Thank you, Beth. It somehow helps that you knew her,' said Albert, quietly. We sat in silence for some time.

'It's getting late, but I'd like to see you again,' said Albert. 'Would you be interested in a walk along the beach one Saturday afternoon?'

'Beach-walking is one of my favourite things.'

We made arrangements and parted.

I sang all the way home.

Our love for each other developed very quickly because we had much in common: a love of the sea, animals, nature, and music. But in many ways we were also very different. I was a committed Christian and rather conservative while Albert was a firm believer in evolution, called himself an agnostic, and was quite alternative in his outlook.

He once asked me, 'Beth, do you believe that if the letters of the alphabet were thrown up in the air and let fall a sufficient number of times, they would eventually produce the complete works of Shakespeare?'

I thought, *This has to be a joke*, so I laughed and answered, 'Of course not!'

Becoming aware of his frosty silence, I glanced at Albert to discover that he was perfectly serious. He replied loftily, 'That shows you have no understanding of the concept of probability.'

I was speechless.

I questioned my suitability for the roles of wife and stepmother—after all, I was forty-six, a spinster who had never been part of a family. Despite our differences, we were certainly in love, and one day we visited a jeweller, selecting a fine sapphire for our engagement ring.

The next question: where should we be married—and by whom?

I did not want to be married in a registry office. Albert couldn't imagine a church wedding.

He was willing for us to be married by the local minister, who had helped the family during Annelore's illness.

We were still undecided, when one day—amid the confusion and noise of the city market—Albert met by chance his friend Dr John. Both were members of the university scuba diving club. After the usual chit-chat, John asked Albert how he and the family were managing.

'I'm engaged to be married,' replied Albert.

'That's good news. Do we know her?'

'No. Her name is Beth Wordie.'

'What a coincidence! We know Beth well,' answered John.

Twenty-seven years earlier, a young woman had come to our home in answer to my mother's newspaper advertisement for a student to rent my room when I left to start my nursing career. Brenda and I became friends. I shared her joy when she married John.

I'd not seen Brenda for thirty years. Now, however, I received a surprise phone call.

'Hello Beth, this is Brenda. John and I are delighted that you and Albert Robertson are to be married. We'd like to give you a wedding reception in our garden—if you would be happy with that.'

'That would be perfect for us. Would it be all right if we were married in your garden, also?'

'Of course it would. We'd love it.'

As a Christian, I had been praying for God's guidance regarding my future. In the way I had met Albert, and in the provision for our marriage, I believed God had given me an answer.

When we discussed a wedding date, Albert said, 'It's a new beginning for us. Let's get married as early as we can in the New Year.'

So our wedding date was set for 2 January 1973. We searched the area for the right place to spend our wedding night and found it: a motel where two tiers of rooms were tastefully set around a swimming pool. We chose a room on the top tier and hugged each other in anticipation.

Albert and Beth Robertson on their wedding day

In 1973, the second day of January was very hot day: 104°F (40°C). I had chosen a pale blue dress with a prettily beaded square neck. Albert looked handsome and very lovable in light brown trousers and a beige shirt. We enjoyed the simple ceremony and the feast set out in the beautiful garden of our hosts. It was quite late when we set out for the motel.

We had just turned off the light when there was a commotion outside our room. The unmistakable clash of bottles—accompanied by heavy breathing as someone lumped up the staircase step by step—was followed by a contented hiccup and the sounds of someone settling down against the wall of our room. The motel staff were long gone. We were 'entertained' by a very drunk man who hiccupped, belched, drank, and sang his way happily through the night. We comforted each other by saying, 'Tomorrow night it will be different.'

The next day, we drove in a leisurely fashion, arriving in Mount Gambier towards evening. We hadn't booked ahead because everyone knew that accommodation there was well-nigh limitless, and it was—except on the night of 3 January 1973! There was a huge conference in progress, and seemingly every spare room in the town was occupied. We drove around for a long time until we found a guesthouse where the lady proprietor at first declined but then took pity on us and offered to help us out.

'You poor dears,' she sympathised, in an accent straight out of Edinburgh. 'Ye'll ne'er find a bed in the Mount and I can't do much, but my daughter has a wee room with a single bed for the lady, and we'll put up a stretcher in the lounge for yer man.'

Albert and I laughed, thanked her, and kissed goodnight, whispering in unison, 'Tomorrow night it will be different!' And it was—we had booked a room in beautiful Lorne before we left Adelaide.

ALBERT WAS A VERY HONEST MAN. I used to appreciate that much more, before I realised he'd be honest with me, too!

'Did you enjoy the meal tonight?' I would question hopefully, and the foolish man would answer.

'I suppose it was all right… but it would have been better if you…' He even vowed and declared his mother made better rice pudding than mine.

'Argh!'

Of course, we had some difficulties. I had been an only child with no experience of close family life, was single into my forties, still unsettled from Africa, menopausal, and trying to be a wife and stepmother.

Albert and I went to a counsellor who was not hopeful. But Albert and I really loved each other—and we would be married for over forty-five years. Albert wanted our relationship to work, and I wanted it to work, too. And it did.

A FEW YEARS AGO, when I answered the phone, someone started singing.

'What are you doing—it's no-one's birthday!'

'It's your forty-fourth wedding anniversary, you silly old thing,' my friend responded enthusiastically.

When I hung up the phone and told Albert what had happened, he put his arm around me and said, 'I'm very glad I met you, Beth.'

'And I'm very glad I met you, too, Albert.'

MY LIFE HAS BEEN CENTRED on the word of God, and I've found that God's prescription for being in relationships with others is opposite to some philosophies. Some say 'maintain the boundaries' and that sort of thing, whereas I don't think that's part of God's plan. I don't think that boundaries are a good idea in lots of ways, because it means that I'm making up my mind that this is the right way to go—and there's no other way. I've decided that this is my choice, and these are my boundaries.

I think unless we get our boundaries from the word of God, we shut people out. God's boundaries are about trying to show love, trying to be polite, not letting the sun go down on our wrath, being the first to make up if we know that our brother or sister has something against us. Counsellors told me that if I followed this way, Albert wouldn't understand and there'd be endless trauma! But what I found was that it set him free to be himself. Not that I've been perfect in all these things; I've been the very opposite.

I've found that when you're in bondage to boundaries, then you put other people in bondage to boundaries, too. With my dear husband, when we were each living in our own camps, sticking to our rights, bad things happened. When I obeyed what I felt to be in the heart of God's Scripture, then I set Albert free, and he did things he'd never thought of doing. We had this joy and this friendship between us. I'm not saying that I have an answer for everyone, but I've found the Word of God to be the 'be all and the end all'. It's the key to being in a relationship, in my opinion.

I'm probably the weakest person the Lord has ever had to manage, because I still have gaps. The nearer you get to the light, the more the spots show. I still have to come back to believing this every day. I still have times when I obviously do the wrong thing.

People still do find me hard to get on with—but I'm not as hard to get on with as I used to be. I believe that I've been set free to talk to people. I feel what I really want now is to pursue love so that people see in me the love of Jesus that reaches out through me to others. I have resentments—things come out that I have to keep giving to God. I wouldn't say that I've arrived in any sense—but living God's philosophy of being in relationship certainly gave me a sense of peace that I didn't have before.

A FRIEND GAVE ME A BOOK—WHICH in itself was quite surprising—and asked, 'If you could choose a person in history that you could be, who would you like to be?' Immediately I thought Mary Magdalene, because she came to the position where she could love God absolutely. I covet that love; I covet that relationship.

I think of being one of the disciples when Jesus said to them, 'You are clean through the Word I have spoken to you, not clean through what you have done. The word I have spoken cleanses.' He was looking at James and John—

who were fighting about who was to be the greatest—and Peter who was going to deny him three times. He looked at them lovingly.

I can't understand the love of God. Jesus says He'll not only present us to the Father—but He'll present each of us with exceeding joy.

11

RETREAT TO THE COUNTRY

It was 1975. We were living at Brighton, in Adelaide near the sea. We had been married for about eighteen months. Two of Albert's children were already married, another shared a house with friends, and Alastair, now fifteen, remained at home with us.

We began to think seriously about moving away from Brighton to a more rural area where we could buy a block of land, plant vegetables, keep ducks, grow native plants and encourage wildlife—and still be close enough to commute to our jobs.

We purchased maps, read the ads in the papers, and looked at a block of land close to the River Murray. We were still exploring our options when a friend invited us to live in her home at Aldinga Beach while she holidayed overseas.

We thoroughly enjoyed exploring the beautiful and diverse region.

Our minds were quickly made up: the area offered more than we had ever dreamed possible. We began a serious search for the ideal block in the Southern Vales region of South Australia—Aldinga, Willunga and McLaren Vale. We began to list the features that appealed to us in each.

'Of course, we can't expect to get everything we want,' said Albert.

'No,' I agreed. 'Let's list the things that are most important to us.'

On a whim, I decided to ring just one more Willunga land agent, just in case.

'Good morning, my name is Beth Robertson. My husband and I are looking to buy a block of land in the area. Could you tell me what you have available please?'

A man named Colin answered. 'Perhaps it would be easier if you could tell me exactly what you want—we have quite a selection of blocks on our books.'

'Well, we've seen several properties and listed the things we liked about them. Are you ready? We'd like a property of about twenty acres with a deep creek and big gum trees. We'd like springs that run all year, two or three acres of almond trees, and a place with a good panoramic view for the house.'

I waited for Colin to laugh. But he didn't.

'We have exactly what you want, Mrs Robertson. The advertisement will be in tomorrow's paper—and the first person to see it will buy it. It's the best block around here.'

'That's exciting. Is there any chance we could come down and see it late this afternoon?'

Five hours later, Albert and I were sitting in the quaint nineteenth-century Alma Hotel, sipping our sherries and looking at each other with bright-eyed wonder. Never had we imagined owning such an incredible block of land! The one-hundred-year-old gate opened into three acres of almond trees; the creek, deep and carpeted with watercress, was overlooked by innumerable huge red gums and leafy acacias; familiar and unfamiliar birdcalls taunted us. Situated on the Willunga hills-face, the land rose reasonably steeply throughout its five-hundred-metre length. There was ample room for a house with a panoramic view towards the ocean.

We built our house and moved in—and would be still happily living there more than forty years later.

THE THREE OF US, Albert, Alastair and I, all loved dogs and we had a succession of them; at one time we had three at the same time. They added to our happiness and the richness of our lives on the block—and improved our fitness levels. By trial and error, we found the dogs we really liked were often German shepherds.

There was Sheba, an RSPCA rescue dog. One ear was up, the other down; she looked as if she were asking a question. She'd been abandoned by her former owners, had spent months in a small cage in the RSPCA, and was now in danger of being put down.

We saw she was loving and intelligent. We answered her questioning gaze with a unanimous yes. When we let her out of the car, she looked at the open spaces and sighed a huge sigh of contentment.

Then there was Grace, a German shepherd puppy. She had belonged to a man that used to take her to the pub. He had an artificial leg, and he often seemed to step on her—she was such a tiny little thing. He decided we could have her. She was a beautiful dog; she grew into a big dark German shepherd with a beautiful coat. She used to smile like a human being—very comical; it looked as if she had false teeth.

She hated to be bathed. Although I tried to put it out of my mind she always seemed to know when it was 'Grace-bath-time'. When I called her, she'd look at me with this great apologetic grin, then turn her back and walk down to the creek and get lost for an hour or two. It never failed. I tried not to think of it, to not suggest a bath, but she always knew…

Our most empathetic dog was Keltie, also a puppy from the RSPCA. Keltie grew to adore Albert and may well have saved his life.

Beth and Albert's beloved German shepherd

Albert, a former Londoner, who had sympathy for animals like snakes, walked around at the height of summer in his thongs. One day he was backing down the steep, narrow path into the creek in his thongs. Keltie came and stood behind him, and wouldn't let him go any further. Albert growled at the dog and the dog stood still, refusing to move, and growled back. Albert looked behind him and realised that he had been just about to step backwards very close to a red-bellied black snake. What amazing behaviour Keltie had exhibited. He knew Albert was in danger. He didn't bark and arouse the snake, and though he was usually a very obedient dog, he had worked out when to disobey.

THERE WERE many things we enjoyed about our block. One of the things that made me happiest was my mother's joy in visiting us. I can picture it now: my mother sitting on a chair in the middle of the orchard, sniffing the clean air as it swept over gum trees and picking up the fragrance of the grasses. She delighted in sitting and husking almonds. She had so longed to return to England with its fields and the scent of new-mown hay. I had never been able to help her return to England, but maybe this was the next best thing.

When she became incapable of caring for herself at home, she moved into a nursing home. Albert and I made the long trip to visit her multiple times. On one visit, he joked with her and as we left, she stood in the passage outside her room, laughing and waving.

A week later, a police car pulled up at our block of land and the policeman came towards us. By the solemn look on his face, I knew that he had come with bad news.

'Are you Elizabeth Robertson?'

'Yes, I am.'

'I am sorry to inform you that your mother

passed away this morning at the nursing home. They would like you to ring them as soon as possible.'

Although we are all aware that our parents' deaths are inevitable, nothing can really prepare us for the pain and the stab of bereavement brought by such news. I rang the nursing home to learn that my mother had been walking in the garden when she suffered a fatal heart attack, and died within a few moments.

At the funeral parlour I was touched at the smallness of her body, its stillness and the coldness of her cheek. When the attendant who had left me to mourn returned to the room and offered me her wedding ring, I refused to take it. My mother had lost everything else she had treasured, and I was determined that she would keep her wedding ring.

A FEW YEARS LATER, Victor Harbor hospital rang me to say that my dad was ill. Albert and I spent some hours with him—he was quite bright and in possession of all his senses. He had been baptised at the age of eighty-three, and had a love for the Bible. I spent time quoting Jesus' words from the Gospel of John (14:2–3): 'In My Father's house are many mansions and I go to prepare a place for you... I will come again and receive you unto Myself so that you may be with Me forever.'

When the doctor came, he listened to Dad's heart and lungs.

'His heartbeat is very strong. I think he is going to recover from this,' said the doctor.

It was getting very late, so Albert and I decided to go home, a journey of about forty minutes. Albert had decided to take the dogs for a walk, and I had begun to get ready for bed when the phone rang.

The hospital staff had rung to let me know that my dad had just died.

At his funeral the coffin was draped with the national flag in recognition of his military service in France during World War I.

It was precious to me to have been with my dad so close to his end and to see him at peace. I realised that his death might have been very different.

12

ENCOUNTER

In the late 1970s, Albert and I went on a holiday to the Flinders Ranges with friends. We pitched our blue tent in the shade of the towering eucalypts that typify the area.

My reading matter for the trip was an autobiography of Maria Von Trapp, entitled *Maria*. I settled down in the tent by myself one afternoon and began to read. It was certainly not what I had expected, but as I read, I was at first engrossed and then envious as Maria described how her life had been transformed by experiencing what some call 'the baptism with the Holy Spirit'.

As the book described the fruit of love, joy and peace that graced her life, my heart cried out for the same. Although the Bible had become the template for my life, something was lacking. Where was my joy and peace?

As I knelt to pray, it seemed that the atmosphere within the tent, already softened by the blue light from its walls, took on a holiness one might experience in a sacred place.

'Father, if this is the way for me to go, please put me in touch with some charismatic Christians.'

God answered my cry when, two days later, I received a phone call from Shirley, with whom I had studied social work at Adelaide University. She and her husband, Jim, now lived and worked in Perth in the social work field. Our conversation went something like this:

'Jim and I are in Adelaide for a conference, and we are hoping to catch up with you.'

'Hello Shirley, good to hear you are in Adelaide. Is there a social work conference I am not aware of?'

After a slight hesitation, Shirley answered, 'It's not a social work conference. It's a charismatic conference.'

Hiding my surprise, for I had considered them to be very traditional in their beliefs, I asked eagerly, 'Is it possible that I could go with you? It's exactly what I have been praying for!'

'Of course you can. We'd be delighted. The meetings are held at Adelaide University. We can pick you up if you like.'

Just a day or so later, I was sitting with an expectant crowd of people waiting for the meeting to begin, not knowing what to expect.

There had been much bitter controversy in Christian circles about what became known as the 'Charismatic Renewal', and some mainline churches split up at this time. I was cautious, but driven by the desire for a vibrant relationship with God.

The meeting was much more animated than I expected, with much audience participation, but the sincerity of the praise and worship was infectious.

Eventually the speaker, James 'Jim' Spillman, was introduced, and I listened avidly to the story of his involvement with the Charismatic Renewal.

Jim, a pastor of a huge American church, had not appreciated the new movement in the church and had spoken vehemently against it. In particular, he had been opposed to the ministry of Kathryn Kuhlman, of whom it was said that more miracles occurred through her ministry than any other evangelists of the day.

Jim apparently thought her results might be due to witchcraft. He was horrified when his own church, ignoring his advice, voted to invite Kathryn to hold a convention there. He described the day of her first meeting when he had hidden amongst the crowd in the balcony.

Worse was to follow as Kathryn proclaimed, 'There is someone in the balcony being healed of a stomach ulcer,' and James felt a significant change take place in his own body. He had been in pain for years and every insurance company he had approached had turned him down. He determined to say nothing about his healing, and sat tight when Miss Kuhlman asked for the person who had been healed to come down to the platform. But Miss Kuhlman's helper realised the truth, and James was marched down from the gallery through the church as his congregation exploded with laughter. Later, he went back to the insurance company and qualified for a million-dollar policy if he wanted it—he declined.

As I listened to James Spillman's testimony, I found the Jesus I had heard about in the New Testament, the Jesus I yearned for in the Sudan. At the end of the meeting an invitation was given for those who wished a prayer for the Baptism of the Holy Spirit. As I joined this prayer I began to speak quietly in tongues.

After the charismatic conference, I had a sense of the Holy Spirit being alive in me in a different way. There followed a new fervour: an increased expectation that I would receive those things promised in the Scriptures, that I would participate in the signs and wonders that Jesus' followers experienced. I felt so much freer.

After that, unless I was talking about God it

was boring; there was something missing. We don't live in a universe that God set going and then stepped back and just let it go without caring about what happens. God's given us the chance to have hands-on, too. God gave us this beautiful world to care for and serve. God trusted us with everything God made and pronounced as perfect. Isn't God amazing?

THIS ENCOUNTER with the Holy Spirit was the beginning of a season of refreshment and renewal. I had a new ease in talking about the Lord. I began asking mothers with young children if I they would like me to bless their babies. Their eagerness to agree filled me with delight: God was using me to bless these little ones in the name of Jesus.

Around 2008, I attended a meeting in Morphett Vale Baptist Church. The speaker, Danny Steyne, asked those aged eighty years or more to stand in order to receive a Jacob blessing from the Lord. Of all the approximately four hundred people present, I stood alone!

Danny then spoke directly to me, the only one over eighty, stating that he had a Jacob blessing for me. I thought to myself, *That'd be right*—I never had been too keen on Jacob, the twister and cheat. I also decided it was an apt anointing for me: I had been an expert liar and cheat in my earlier life—and I still had a few problems when tempted! However, God had transformed Jacob—and had changed his name to Israel to underline him being a 'new creation' by God's grace. I hoped that God would change me, too. God didn't need to change my name—Elizabeth means 'house of God'.

I do believe there was a change in my ability to witness—though there were still many flaws in me. God calls the weak and the nothings by the world's standards, so that those who are forgiven much may love more (Luke 7:47). I definitely qualified on the weakness scale! Oh, but how I longed for that 'measure of the fullness of the stature of Christ' to which Jesus called me, knowing that without Jesus I could do nothing and with Jesus I could do 'all things' (Philippians 4:13).

13

BEGINNING A NEW JOURNEY

It was in 1982 that the doors of the Noarlunga Health Centre closed firmly behind me for the last time. I was a retiree at age fifty-six.

After thirty years in the workforce following my time in Africa, I was free to pursue my personal interests.

When the going was tough, I had occasionally rehearsed this day in my mind, with joy—but where had the joy gone now that my 'working life' really was over?

Would there be a real purpose to my life? How would I fill my days?

It was as if my job as a social worker had defined me as a person. Without it, nonentity stared me in the face.

The first days were occupied with the tasks

that accompany retirement—one of which was to visit the superannuation officer. As he consulted my lists of figures, his brow creased and I became concerned. He hesitated, scratching his head. My concern mounted as I awaited his verdict.

Finally, leaning back in his chair and, with a dazed look on his face, he remarked, 'I have never ever seen a superannuation claim like yours. There have been many unpredictable changes in our system, but it seems as if you had inside knowledge, and you qualified every time by the skin of your teeth. When I think how little you've contributed and how much you're going to get out of your super, I can say only one thing: someone up there loves you!'

'You're right,' I answered. 'Someone up there does love me.'

I READ THE ELECTRIFYING, often spine-chilling adventures of Andrew Bilj, *God's Smuggler* (Brother Andrew 1955), who risked his life taking Bibles into communist countries during the Cold War. It convinced me that divine miracles still occur. And, for me, fiction breathed its last as my favourite read; fiction was finally trumped by truth. I threw out hundreds of books: mysteries, thrillers, love stories…

Discovering that my Chinese brothers and

sisters were hungering for the Scriptures that were my daily food affected me so greatly that I grasped the opportunity to take Bibles to China. I was involved in an act that, at the time, was against the wishes of the Chinese government but not unlawful.

I joined a group of six who travelled together from Australia to Hong Kong. We split up for the trip from Hong Kong into China, each travelling singly by train. I loved the experience: the unfamiliar green paddy fields with their stooping straw-hatted labourers; trying to talk with the friendly, smiling people in the carriage who'd never heard of Australia. We managed to exchange some information with much laughter and arm-waving, but their main focus was buying duty-free cigarettes.

Waiting in customs at the border, a peace descended as if I were in a rose garden. This was strange because the Chinese officials had gathered around a young German woman, and were shouting and poking their fingers at words in the one book in her possession. I have no idea what the book was about. The woman was obviously afraid: she was crying. I observed that the senior official—a grim-faced older woman—was staring at me fixedly as if measuring my reactions. I remained enveloped in my heavenly rose garden and was beckoned through without a hitch. I prayed the prayer offered up by Brother Andrew whenever he was in a similar situation: 'Lord, make seeing eyes blind.' I put my case through the X-ray machine with my left hand; the case in my right hand, containing the Bibles, was apparently invisible.

In February 2017—nearly thirty years after my visit to China—I was in hospital, this time with a suspected heart problem.

'Come in,' I said in response to a knock on the door of my hospital room.

'Good afternoon, Mrs Robertson. I've come to take your blood pressure,' said the nurse, a Chinese woman named Amy, who radiated a quiet friendliness. We were soon engaged in an I'd-like-to-get-to-know-you conversation. I told her that I had been born in Australia but that my grandfather had come from Jamaica, then asked her about her homeland.

'I was born in a little village not far from Beijing,' said Amy.

'I visited China nearly thirty years ago and found it a very beautiful and interesting country,' I said, without revealing the fact that I had visited China in order to carry Bibles to Chinese Christians. 'I was very surprised to see so much open land in a country with such a large population.'

'It has changed a lot since those days,' Amy

remarked. 'Our village is now part of Beijing and my mother lives in a forty-storey housing block. There are fifteen steps between each floor and sometimes the lifts don't work. When this happens, people who are at home don't go out and those who are not at home stay in a hotel—too many steps to climb. There are many, many people everywhere now.'

'I suppose that's why the government brought in the "one child" policy.'

'Yes. I am forty-five now, the sixth child in our family, and that law came in shortly after I was born. It was an evil policy. Every family wanted to have a son and the girls were killed or aborted. Now there are millions of men—and no women for them to marry.'

As Amy unwound the cuff from my arm, she noticed my Bible and remarked, 'I am a Christian too.'

'Then we are sisters,' I laughed as we hugged each other. 'How did you become a Christian?'

'My mother was given a Bible and heard a man speak about Jesus, and she became a believer. I was working in Beijing and when I came home I found a paper in my mother's room with some good words that I had never heard before. They said that if I had everything—all the clothes, all the money, and all the desirable things in the world—they would do me no good in the end without Jesus.'

'So, Amy, you became a Christian because of the words you read from the Bible?'

As she answered, her eyes were closed, her voice softened. 'Yes—because I had never heard such beautiful words.'

'It interests me because it was nearly thirty years ago that I read how much the Christians in your country needed Bibles and that's why I went to China: to take some with me. The Chinese officials didn't approve and would take the Bibles if they found them. Where is your mother now?'

'She's still in the same place in China. And she still writes words from the Bible on pieces of paper and hands them out to people in the market. Things are easier in China now for Christians—about thirty Christians meet in our apartment for church each week.'

Although it is most unlikely that Amy's story and mine are connected—that the Bible her mother had read was one I had taken—I could believe that as Amy and her family had found spiritual life through the reading of the word of God, others may have been given the same opportunity through the Bibles I had been privileged to deliver nearly thirty years earlier.

WHEN I WAS in my sixties, I visited England and America. While I was waiting on a train platform, a lady and two little children stood beside me.

She was a small, slight Scottish woman, with a very sweet face and a lovely complexion. We soon started talking. She told me that she'd just lost her husband. We started talking about God, and the Holy Spirit flooded us. It was as if the Lord wrapped us around with his love. I remember us hugging each other. We repeated the Aaronic Prayer together: 'The Lord bless you and keep you, the Lord make his face to shine on you and be gracious to you. The Lord lift up his countenance upon you and give you peace.'

On another occasion, I got lost in London, while walking around all the places that I knew and liked from playing Monopoly as a child. I was very near The Angel, Islington, when I met a dear English lady, petite with white hair and beautiful skin. We began talking. She was a Christian, and I called her my 'little angel' at The Angel, Islington.

My little angel directed how to get to different places and led me around to some of them. And all the time we walked, we talked. She told me how sad it had been during the war, and about the terrible times of the bombings of London. As we talked together, the Lord comforted us. We hugged each other. We were one in the Lord yet so different in everything else. As we parted we made an arrangement to meet before the throne of grace in heaven.

I had booked the cheapest possible tour of Scotland. The bus on which we travelled was elderly and unreliable. We came to a humped bridge and, the bus being low, the undercarriage was caught and we ended up see-sawing on the bridge. It was very good for us, as instead of rushing through the countryside we were able to spend several hours, apparently where Prince Charles took his skiing holidays amongst the heather.

In America, I visited Sam and Mary-Helen, and Geraldine: my fellow missionaries in the Sudan. Sam and Mary-Helen had received a letter for me from their son, David—the baby with whom she had been pregnant when I visited Yabus Bridge, who was by then a missionary in India. 'What do you say to someone who saved your life,' he wrote in his letter. His parents believed that the bed rest, and going home to the States immediately, were instrumental, under God's care, in Mary-Helen maintaining her pregnancy.

When I visited Geraldine, she complained about the pain in her arthritic feet.

Suddenly, I received a mind picture in which I knelt in front of her, took her feet in my hands, and prayed for her healing.

'Was that vision really from you, God?' I

asked anxiously, knowing that many people have great reservations on the subject of healing miracles in the present day. Eventually, I did exactly what I had seen in the vision. Gerry said nothing at the time, but three months later she wrote and told me that the Lord had healed her at that time —all praise to Him.

14

ADELAIDE ANECDOTES

The brightly lit bus lumbered to a halt to admit my friend Janet and myself, as we began the sixty-kilometre journey home following a meeting. It was late in the evening, and we could understand the look of relief on the face of the bus driver, who had been dauntingly alone in the immense articulated vehicle. We pocketed our tickets and sat down, three rows back on the right-hand side of the bus, and the bus continued its rocky journey.

As the doors swung open at the next stop, we heard a loud commotion: shouting, laughter and the rattle of cans. Two young men were struggling up the bus steps with a large cardboard carton of alcoholic drinks. It was obvious that they had already sampled a significant number of these cans, and were now uproariously drunk.

Finally, they juggled the tray into the bus, received their tickets from the now quaking bus driver, exchanged a conspiratorial glance with each other, and sat down directly opposite us. Ignoring the driver's protests, they proceeded to talk as loudly as possible, using as many expletives as they could summon up, and stealing the odd glance at us to note our reactions.

I'm still not sure what made me do it, but I took a deep, diaphragmatic breath, opened my mouth and, summoning the decibels of a former public speaker and songstress, bellowed forth:

'Amazing grace how sweet the sound that saved a wretch like me…'

At this point Janet, who has a very fine soprano voice and almost as many decibels as me, joined me. I dropped down to sing alto.

We hadn't got very far when silence from the boys exploded like a clap of thunder in the bus. The driver took a quick look over his shoulder. The two young men sat open-mouthed.

One of them, whom I will call Sam, blurted out, 'What church do you go to?'

'A church in Willunga,' I responded.

Sam then told us his story, that he used to attend one of the largest churches in Adelaide and had even been a youth leader but had turned his back on this. His companion, whom I will call James, seemed surprised when Sam told us, 'My mother still prays for me.'

'Your mother prays for you, Sam!' said James. 'That's cool man, cool.'

During the rest of the journey Sam was occupied in trying to remember choruses that we could all sing. The two young men departed quietly from the bus a few stops later.

I have often thought of the two young men and joined my prayers with Sam's mother.

But I would love to have been a fly on the wall to hear what the bus driver told his wife.

As my Penguin Club colleague Jan and I stepped from the shadowy hall after our meeting into the bright summer sunlight and approached my car, we noticed a small heap of shattered glass lying on the ground alongside.

'Oh no!' exclaimed Jan. 'I think your car's been broken into.'

'Well, if you're right, whoever it was will be badly disappointed. There was nothing in there worth stealing.'

I was both right and wrong in my assumption. Certainly, there had been nothing in the car to attract a thief. Nevertheless, my ponderous black leather New King James Bible had vanished.

'You don't seem too concerned,' remarked Jan. 'I'd be furious if it were me.'

'I've changed a bit lately,' I answered hesitantly. 'There's a verse in the Bible that tells us to give thanks in every circumstance—because God is working to use what happens to us, for our good.'

'I'll be waiting to see what He does with this!' said Jan.

There was one immediate problem, however. I was leaving early the next morning for a Bible conference in Naracoorte Southeast, and you can't attend a Bible conference without a respectable Bible. It was then I remembered the Salvation Army op shop down the road. If I hurried, I could reach it before closing time.

The Salvo officer greeted me with sympathy, but apologised that the only Bible available was a children's Bible—the Good News version.

Good, though not what I would've chosen. I looked at the vivid picture on the cover and noted the pristine condition. It was a children's Bible, but it was certain no child had ever opened it. The flyleaf was blank.

'We don't charge for Bibles,' said the Salvo officer with a smile.

I thanked him, took the Bible and went on my way. Two days later, at the Bible conference, I was seated beside a serenely beautiful lady from Ghana in Africa, elegant in her blue and purple gown and matching head tie.

The teaching that morning had centred

around the idea that we can be led by God in our relationship with others—even total strangers.

As a demonstration, the presenter said, 'I want you to pray now and ask God what you should do for the person seated next to you. When you receive an answer, speak to your neighbour about it.'

As I prayed, I became aware of exactly what I should do. I turned to the lady next to me, saying, 'I believe God wants me to give you this Bible.'

As she reached out her hand for the Bible, she seemed first amazed and then tearful. She explained, 'Just last night my husband and I were talking, and he said we must buy Bibles for our three daughters, and when we do, we should get them the Good News versions. God must have heard, but tell me—where did you find this Bible?'

'Well,' I started to explain, 'that's quite a story…'

THE SPECIALIST RIFFLED through the pages of reports, put down his pen and cleared his throat. I braced myself to hear the words I feared—

'Mrs Robertson, I'm sorry to tell you that you are suffering from Parkinson's Disease.'

The diagnosis was not really a surprise. I was

a trained nurse and had been trying to ignore the way my thumbs and fingers made pill-rolling movements and my body trembled inside my skin.

Adelaide's 'best' specialist in Parkinson's Disease then subjected me to hours of testing of every kind. I drew, calculated, spoke, walked, fell backwards, was examined physically and digitally. There was no doubt in the specialist's opinion.

Over the next two years the symptoms increased. I had several falls, could no longer play tennis, became fearful of crossing the street, developed severe tremors in my left hand periodically and felt a constant shaking of my body.

As I prayed, I felt comforted but still concerned for the future, until it was impressed on me that I only need live one day at a time. I wanted to trust God for that.

In April 2013, I learned from a friend that healing meetings were being held about sixty kilometres from my home and that a bus was going from our area. Would I be interested in going? I certainly was. The evangelist Jeff Jensen from the USA had been used of God to perform many miracles.

The three hundred people in the meeting hall sang fervently to strummed guitars and beaten drums for what seemed a very long time, but at last Jeff Jensen stood to speak. Our faith increased as he testified to the miraculous events occurring overseas as well as in Australia. He asked for testimonies from people who had been healed, and among those who spoke was a friend of mine who testified to the healing of a carpal tunnel problem.

The meeting quietened as Jeff stood for several minutes, looking around the room and muttering to himself, 'Roberts, Roberts, Roberts.' Then he said, 'Will you please come out the front?'

Not really certain he meant me, I faltered, 'Who? Me?'

'Yes, you. I believe you need healing.'

'I do, I have Parkinson's Disease.'

'I have seen the Lord heal Parkinson's Disease. What is your name?'

'My name is Elizabeth,' I answered.

'Elizabeth what? Is it Roberts?' asked Jeff.

'It's Robertson,' I answered, astonished.

'God has given me part of your name so that you would believe. Do you believe that God will heal you?'

As he spoke, a quiet 'knowing' engulfed me and I answered, 'Yes, I believe.' I was so thankful that the Lord, who knows my tendency to doubt, supplied two miracles—the giving of my name as well as the healing.

Every symptom of the disease left me at that moment and has never returned.

15

A TURNING POINT

I needed a new interest, but at eighty-seven what could I do?

I had been wonderfully healed of the Parkinson's Disease which had been diagnosed three years earlier by the best doctors in Adelaide. I no longer suffered from the periodic tremor in my left arm, my body no longer shook imperceptibly within my skin, and I no longer dreaded crossing the street. I had fallen three times just prior to my healing, but for several months there had been no further falls. I no longer anticipated a life of rapid decline.

While I was considering my limited options, a pamphlet arrived from Koorong bookshop. I was about to throw it out when I caught sight of an advertisement. The Christian college, Tabor, situated at Millswood in Adelaide, was offering a postgraduate course in creative writing.

I screwed up the pamphlet and threw it away, but the thought kept niggling, so much so that I wondered if God might have some purpose in it. I know it sounds presumptuous to think that the mighty Creator of the cosmos could possibly care or have a plan for an insignificant octogenarian.

There were many insuperable barriers. I had no way of getting there. I couldn't afford it. I might have written good essays at school—seventy-five years ago! My computer skills were miniscule. But the thought wouldn't be banished.

One morning after church I heard a young woman talking to a friend about her intention to study teaching at Tabor College that year. I found myself saying, 'I heard about a course in creative writing that sounded interesting, but I could never afford it.'

'But you don't have to pay for it until you are earning a good wage,' chimed the girls.

'That sounds too good to be true. Surely it wouldn't apply to an oldie like me. How would I get there?'

'We are sure it would, and you could come with us.'

'But don't they use computers?'

Another barrier crashed when I met a friend of a friend, Rob Renshaw, the perfect combination of patient saint (available online all hours) and computer genius. Rob continued to enable me to do the impossible—like write a book.

TWO YEARS LATER, looking out into the quadrangle of the college I saw Belay, an Ethiopian scholar now living in Australia and studying at Tabor College to be a pastor. I could see him sitting on the chair enjoying the sunlight and warmth of an early spring day.

Reflecting on the past, I began to wonder how the people in Africa to whom we had been ministering now felt about our mission work. It occurred to me that I could ask Belay his opinion. During the years I spent working in Africa in the 1950s, I had been stationed in the Sudan near the border of Ethiopia. We used to go to Ethiopia for holidays because of its high altitude; it was many degrees cooler in temperature than the Sudan.

As I approached, Belay graciously put down the work he was studying.

'Belay, can I ask you a question please?'

'Yes of course,' he answered with a warm smile.

'I would like to know what you think now about the work done by missionaries like me in your country. Is there lasting benefit?'

Belay looked thoughtful and was silent for a

time before replying. 'We had our own religion—'

I interrupted. 'Was that the Coptic church?'

'Yes, but we didn't understand it very well. The priests spoke in a language we didn't understand, and it was very formal. When the Protestant missionaries came, they taught us differently. We all make mistakes, and the missionaries too may have made mistakes, but you shouldn't worry about that. God has taken care of us, and from that time many people love Jesus. The important thing is that we now know Jesus in our hearts. I spent some time in prison, and although it was very hard, my joy was much greater than the pain. Although it is good to live here, I wish I could go back to Ethiopia and tell my people about Jesus' love.'

I had often wondered about the legacy we had left behind—especially since so many Christians in the Sudan died for their faith. There was such warmth and love in Belay's face as he spoke to me that it really reassured me.

In researching the book, we found that the Uduks I loved so much were not totally wiped out by the troubles in Sudan but were persecuted and scattered to bear a valiant Christian testimony as refugees in different places, including Uganda, Ethiopia, Khartoum and a few in the United States. Some are now returning to Chali and their other homelands, and Christian churches are beginning to flourish in the area. The Uduks have won respect and admiration for their courage and vibrant Christian faith in all these places.

It began as a very ordinary day, that day in 2016, the year I turned ninety. My friend Vivian had graciously offered to help me once again with the writing of my spiritual memoir.

As I sat by the window of Tabor College cafe, while the sun chased the last of the shadows of night away, Vivian appeared, and we were chatting brightly as she unpacked her bag, pulling forth pages of printed material.

Smiling, she dropped the bombshell. 'I've found something extraordinary. A friend of mine researched the story of your grandfather, Vaules Wordie.'

My heart sank. I was stunned and angry.

My grandfather had been a wispy shadow that had darkened all of my life. No-one had ever spoken to me about him. I had grown up knowing there was something different about me, and it wasn't a good thing, and it was somehow connected to my Jamaican heritage. I used to come home from school, crying, because the other children called me names.

I had spent my whole life fearing what I

might hear about my grandfather. Where ignorance is bliss, it's folly to be wise.

I discovered I had a reason to be proud, not a reason to cower. My grandfather was much respected and loved to help people. Everything I held dear, he held dear. If I could have chosen someone to be a forebear, I would have chosen someone with all his qualities: he loved the Bible, loved the Lord, was eloquent in his preaching, loved people. It was almost as though my grandfather came alive to me for the first time. I came to feel a warmth towards him, as a friend.

Of all my known ancestors I am now proudest of Vaules Augustus Wordie, my grandfather, who died twenty-one years before my birth. His obituary tells of a gracious, well respected Christian man. He stood up for his principles and carried the argument for racial acceptance to the parliament of the day.

We found these mentions in newspapers.

> 'In the death of Mr. Vaules A. Wordie, which occurred on Thursday, there has passed a noted personality in Adelaide. The deceased gentleman's colour—he was of negro descent—distinguished him no more than his kind and courteous manner and his deep concern for the happiness of others. Although possessed of a fervid

religious nature, he was an extraordinarily entertaining companion, and nobody more heartily appreciated or enjoyed innocent amusement. For many years he was on the Adelaide Methodist local preachers' list, and frequently conducted services. He had a fine delivery and a splendid vocabulary, and invested his utterances with a feeling and sincerity which always appealed forcefully to his audience. For nearly a quarter of a century he was a teacher at the Pirie Street Methodist Sunday School, where his gentle spirit and loving regard for their welfare greatly endeared him to the scholars. In addition to teaching, he had charge of the Sunday School library. His culture manifested itself in various ways, particularly in connection with literary work. He was a Vice-President of the Pirie Street Literary Society, and for a long period both by precept and example assisted materially to develop in his fellows a love for literature of an inspiring and educational character. He often contributed essays and criticisms which bore the impress of literary skill, and a few years ago won first prize in an impromptu debate contest, and for an essay in connection with the south Australian Literary Society's annual competitions. The subject of the latter was, "The White Australia Problem." Mr. Wordie also took a keen interest in friendly society matters, and rendered much valuable help to different organisations. He was a Past President of the Cosmopolitan Friendly Benefit society, a P.G. of the Adelaide Lodge of Oddfellows, M.U., a member of the Grand Lodge of the Loyal Orange Institution, the Loyal Harmony Lodge, and the Protestant Defence Association. The deceased gentleman who was held in the highest respect by a wide circle of friends and acquaintances, was 54 years of age, and has left a widow and a large family of young children.'

— *THE REGISTER*, SATURDAY, 28 DECEMBER 1907

'The Legislative Council was content to meet on Tuesday afternoon at the usual time. A novel petition was introduced by the Hon. J. Warren from Augustus Vaules Wordie, praying that he might be heard at the bar of the Council in objection to the Coloured Immigration Restriction Bill. The petition was received.'

— *ADELAIDE OBSERVER*, 19 DECEMBER 1896

TRANSITION, the process of changing from one condition to another, has been a hallmark of my life: spiritual, geographic, professional, and psychological. Apart from the transition to Christianity, one of the greatest of these transitions was the change from the shame and loathing I had felt—because of the racism I encountered—towards my Jamaican heritage.

With eternal thanks to God, to my longsuffering tutors, to Tabor and to the Australian taxpayers, I satisfactorily completed the Tabor course a month or two before my ninetieth birthday.

Beth with her husband Albert on her graduation from Tabor College

Beth on her ninetieth birthday with her husband, Albert

16

HEARTBROKEN BUT HOMEWARD BOUND

Towards the end of 2018 it became obvious that both Albert and I were failing in health and energy, requiring much government assistance in addition to that which was provided by family and friends.

Despite the help, life was difficult. I experienced some heart and bowel problems, but the main change was in Albert who lost his appetite for food and fluids. He became increasingly weak as he approached his ninety-eighth birthday on the fourth of March 2019.

Thankfully, he made the day and was happy in the presence of the family. He and I grew closer together as the days passed.

In the middle of one night in May, I was awakened by the light shining in Albert's room. When I went to check on him, he complained of chest pains. An ambulance was called, which took us to Flinders Medical Centre. The verdict was 'a minor heart attack', and he was sent home. However, later that evening the hospital discovered that a mistake had been made; the damage to Albert's heart had been very serious and he was advised to return to the hospital. Even so, he chose to remain at home.

Early in June, he was readmitted to hospital. When it became obvious that he had only a few days to live, we decided to look for a large room in a nursing home where members of Albert's family could visit and where I could also live, in order to nurse him. This plan worked.

Albert finally passed away on the twelfth of June, 2019. The funeral bore tribute to an honest and sincere man. His ashes were scattered on the land we loved and shared.

JUNE FADED INTO JULY, and I remained in the room where Albert had died—wondering what would happen to me.

One thing was certain: I could not return to the home Albert and I had loved for forty-five years. The house was too isolated for me to live there alone. A great concern was our beautiful golden Labrador, Cheetah, elderly with soulful brown eyes. My friend Janet stepped in and gave him two happy years where he became known as 'Wonky', the benign ruler of Janet's garden, presiding over the rampant red-combed rooster, the large fluffy cat, and a tribe of lively chickens.

As I prayed, I believed I should move nearer to Adelaide. I had already received much assistance and advice from Albert's family. One night, I sat at my computer in the same nursing home which was unsuitable for my future, and made a list of preferable nursing homes. There was no doubt which one appealed most. At 2 am I went to sleep, and at 8 am was wakened by my insistent mobile phone.

It was my stepdaughter-in-law. 'There are two vacancies in that nursing home we visited recently. Are you interested?'

'Yes, very. I decided just a few hours ago to go there.'

The room offered was spacious, with a delightful view through a leafy garden onto a quiet street, and across the road to a wonderfully constructed nineteenth-century church.

Apart from two short visits, including one for the auction day, I never did return home.

A local land agent did such a wonderful job that when I was asked for a reference, I wrote that my whole family would definitely have awarded him eleven out of ten. The money received from the sale of the block matched exactly the costs of the room.

I moved in shortly afterward and was blessed to find myself living in a well-kept and friendly nursing home. Adjusting was not always easy, but with much help from staff, family and friends, I slowly started to settle in. Since moving into the nursing home, I've realised that many of my carers come from other countries—India, China, Cambodia, Nepal, the Philippines, and others. When I feel like complaining, I try to recall what some of them have lost and suffered.

It was in the evening after an uneventful day that I discovered I was bleeding copiously from the bowel. I was soon on my way by ambulance to the 'new' Royal Adelaide Hospital.

It was a busy time for the emergency department and there were at least seven other ambulances 'ramped' outside, awaiting a vacancy for their patient. The cramped ambulance was hot and uncomfortable, and I was grateful that my wait was less than an hour.

After an examination, I was transferred to a single bedroom in a ward, to live on ice chips while my fate was decided.

My doctor told me later that I had lost the equivalent of four packs of blood. I was too weak for surgery under a general anaesthetic, and a blood transfusion would not solve the problem. My life was in considerable danger.

Early on the third day, a doctor came to see me with some questions. Would I want to be resuscitated if I 'died' under treatment? I told him, 'No, I am almost ninety-four.' How would I feel about living life as an invalid? I answered in much the same way.

'Then we have a possible solution, but there are things you should consider. This procedure has not been attempted before. The plan would be to search for the leaking blood vessel, insert a catheter into the groin and burn the offending vein. There's a risk that we might not find the problem, or that we burn your bowel in the process, which could be painful or even life-threatening, or that the procedure is entirely unsuccessful. Please consider carefully.'

I didn't need time to consider. 'My answer is yes. This is the only chance I have.'

'We also believe that,' the doctor said. 'By the way, the procedure will be photographed.'

I was conscious throughout the operation and spent the time imagining I was walking with Jesus on the shores of the Sea of Galilee. The operation was successful.

My local doctor remarked later, 'If you'd gone to any other hospital in the world that day, you probably wouldn't have survived. You realise by now you have a world-famous bowel?'

As I near the end of my life, I see a distinct pattern of God's grace and forgiveness throughout the years; a process of deliverance from darkness into radiance, from hopelessness into hope, a process that began with my conversion to Christ. God has worked so many blessings throughout my life. One of the most special was when I believe the Holy Spirit helped me to find a closeness to God for which I'd longed since I first accepted Jesus as my Lord and Saviour.

Reading the Bible has helped with this. 'In everything give thanks' (1 Thessalonians 5:18).

I've discovered that the Lord doesn't like people to murmur. I'm pretty good at murmuring. In response to the Lord impressing on me the need to have a spirit of gratitude, I wrote a little poem:

> *For, Lord, it is no platitude*
> *to say the grace of gratitude*
> *will sanctify my attitude*
> *creating a beatitude.*

I have written much about the cruelty and rejection I received as a child, but I am also sorrowfully aware that I was sometimes equally cruel to others less fortunate than myself.

Once, when I was about twelve years old, I

was walking with a group of girls by whom I yearned to be accepted. As we walked along, I saw another girl, Joyce, in the distance. Joyce's face was terribly disfigured, and as a result she had few friends. I pretended not to see her—but she obviously realised the truth, and to this day I cannot forget her look of pain. I still weep when I think of it.

I can imagine more than a few people being very surprised that a book has been written about my life, 'after all the mistakes *she's* made'—and they'd be right. My only boast can be in what God has done. I so wish I could ask forgiveness of those I have wronged and wounded.

In his book *Nearing Home*, Billy Graham asks the question I have asked recently of myself: 'What testimony are you passing on to others following you?' He urges us to 'pass on … the truths of God's Word so that younger generations will be as Joshua, filled with the spirit of wisdom.' The same hope underlies my writing of this memoir.

I asked God not so long ago why He had been so kind to me and had chosen me to work for Him. 'I am so weak,' I wailed.

I believe His answer flashed into my spirit. 'It's *because* you are so weak.'

I find that comforting—God is the source of my strength.

Joyous sunlight and soft breezes combined forces, pushing aside the shading leaves of the trees outside my window, to play on the glass and reveal the stately beauty of the nineteenth-century church across the road.

My mind roamed far from my room in the nursing home, happily recalling some of the 'mountain top' experiences of my life where, from my perspective, I had seen the miraculous. A knock at the door interrupted my thoughts.

'Come in,' I called and was pleased when my carer for the day, Naomi, appeared. I already knew we shared a Christian faith. I also knew that Naomi had been born in South Vietnam. As she approached, I remarked, 'Naomi, I believe in miracles.'

'So do I,' she responded with a smile.

'Have you ever experienced one?' I pressed.

'Yes, I have.'

'Please tell me about it.'

I listened avidly and have her permission to share her story with you. She checked it for accuracy.

Naomi began, 'I was born in South Vietnam in 1981, the first child to my Catholic family. It was a lovely place then, like heaven, but it became like hell.

'My father worked for the American Army,

which had come to help fight with Cambodia against North Vietnam. When the Americans left, my father was sent to a concentration camp for ten years.

'It was very hard for my mother. Every night, we slept in a tunnel under our house. The communists would come into the countryside, and every morning there would be many dead. Even girls as young as sixteen would be killed, or sent to Cambodia to fight. Educated people were targets because they were "harder to control" under communism. We were all afraid.

'When I was eighteen years old, and my sister seventeen, our mother used gold left by our father to arrange passage for us as refugees in a boat owned by people smugglers, headed for Malaysia.'

Amazed at Naomi's story, I couldn't help asking, 'Was it a big boat?'

'No, it was a very small fishing boat,' responded Naomi, 'and there were twenty-six people in it.'

'Weren't you scared?' I interjected. 'You must have known that many boats didn't make it.'

'Not really. Anything was safer than home. We thought we would die one way or another.'

'Please tell me more, Naomi.'

'We were on the sea for a month. There were ferocious storms, and it was so slow. Then the boat broke down. We just floated. Our food and water were gone. When drops of water formed on the boat, we would lick them off. We were so hungry, thirsty and afraid.

'One day, as we looked out over the sea, we were frightened to see a place where the water was splashing up high. What was it? Would it hurt us?

'I grew up in the city and had never heard of whales, but a fisherman on the boat told us not to be afraid—that these animals often helped people. They were very big—as big as the boat.'

'How many were there? Did you count them?'

'About ten or twelve whales.'

'Then what happened?'

'They pushed the boat through the water for a long time—about half a day—until we saw an oil tanker far away. When it came near, they noticed the whales and we were all saved. As we left on the tanker, we saw the whales lift themselves up in the water and wave their tails in the air like they were saying goodbye to us.'

Naomi's tears and trembling as she recounted her story testified to the truth of her account. Finally, she turned to me, saying, 'Yes, Beth, I do believe in miracles. I pray and thank God every day.'

You can probably guess my wholehearted response to Naomi's surprising and beautiful story.

Yes, I also believe in miracles.

My story in this book began with a glorious sunset and ends with a radiant morning, and Naomi's miraculous story of the whales. Throughout my life I believe God has been with me. In September 2022 it was eighty years since I dedicated my life to Him, a decision in which I rejoice.

My earliest memory of the Light of Christ was when I was quite small—a picture of Jesus the Good Shepherd, carrying a lamb upon His shoulders. I remember the song, too: *I am Jesus' Little Lamb*. But it wasn't until I turned sixteen that I came to know Jesus as my own Good Shepherd and started to hear His voice calling me to follow, again and again, and in so many surprising ways.

The stories I've written about in this book testify to God's faithfulness and the promise Jesus gave: 'Come unto me, all ye that labour and are heavy laden, and I will give you rest' (Matthew 11:28). How wonderful it is to have such a vision and a hope!

May I continue to listen and to follow, and, as the new dawn breaks, may I answer, 'Yes, Lord, I come.'

ABOUT THE AUTHOR

Elizabeth 'Beth' Robertson nee Wordie (RN, RM, BA, DipSocStud) is a former nurse, missionary and social worker. She lives in Adelaide, South Australia.

www.ingramcontent.com/pod-product-compliance
Lightning Source LLC
Chambersburg PA
CBHW020320010526
44107CB00054B/1911